VICTORIAN AND EDWARDIAN HAMPSTEAD
Alastair Service

With best wishes,

[signature]

28 June 1989

Dedicated to my grandparents
Frank Stanley and
Annie Dollar Service
and
The Ven. Arthur and Viva Sharp
and my parents
Douglas and Evelyn Service,
all of them Hampstead dwellers
between 1890 and 1980.

All royalties from the sales of
this book will be divided
between The Burgh House Trust
and The Victorian Society.

THE ILLUSTRATIONS

The illustration on the front cover shows the home built for Frank Holl at no. 6 Fitzjohn's Avenue (now demolished), and is reproduced by kind permission of the London Borough of Camden. The illustration on the back cover is repeated on p.31. The London Borough of Camden also kindly gave permission to reproduce illustrations 4, 8, 9, 11, 16, 17, 27, 28, 47, 81, 82.

Illustrations 23 and 44 are reproduced by kind permission of the National Portrait Gallery.

Illustrations 7, 10, 36, 43, 60 are from the collection of Historical Publications Ltd. All other illustrations were supplied by the author.

VICTORIAN AND EDWARDIAN HAMPSTEAD
Alastair Service

Two Walks around its Streets and Buildings

with assistance from
John Brandon-Jones, Neil Burton, Stuart Gray,
Edward Hubbard, Ian Norrie, Andrew Saint,
Matthew Saunders, Janet Sondheimer,
Robert Thorne and Christopher Wade.

HISTORICAL PUBLICATIONS

Map of Hampstead 1814

By J. and W. Newton for J. J. Park, 'The topography and natural history of Hampstead'

Introduction

Writing of Hampstead in his memoirs, the distinguished Victorian architect Sir T. Graham Jackson reported in 1905: 'The part where we lived is comparatively little altered externally. Towards London all is new and hideous, but old Hampstead on the hill-top, and between that and Frognal, still retains its shady groves enclosed by rails and gates leading to old-world houses with nice gardens, curious little steep alleys ending in flights of steps upwards or downwards...' Since Jackson had spent much time, two decades earlier, radically altering the interior of the Parish Church, he must have shared the common human characteristic of deploring all change except that which we have brought about ourselves. And although in the late twentieth century we can still identify with his dislike of change, those Victorian and Edwardian streets and buildings, which Jackson regretted, now contribute as much to Hampstead's charm and character as the Georgian houses.

To understand what happened to hilltop Hampstead between 1870 and 1914, it is necessary to know something of the heroic campaign to save Hampstead Heath from development by the owners of its land, the Maryon Wilson family, lords of Hampstead manor from 1707 onwards. Their estate consisted of two major parts (the larger area of 356 acres including most of West Hampstead and stretching up both sides of what is now Fitzjohn's Avenue and Finchley Road to Frognal, then on to Platt's Lane: the smaller part of 60 acres running north from Hampstead ponds across what is now our Heath). The Maryon Wilsons also had manorial rights over other extensive parts of the Heath. The family had a manor house at the north-west angle of Frognal, and Frognal Lane, but leased that to others since they themselves lived at the great Elizabethan Charlton House near Greenwich. In 1829, Sir Thomas Maryon Wilson Bt. sought (unsuccessfully) the first of a series of Private Acts of Parliament to allow him to build on his estate and on the Heath. A long battle started, with the banker John Gurney Hoare leading the opposition from the 1850s onwards, and the Commons Preservation Society from 1865, until Sir Thomas died in 1869. His brother and heir Sir John, to everyone's exhausted relief, sold the Heath properties to the Metropolitan Board of Works in 1872 and the cause was won — though another campaign (led by Sir George Shaw-Lefevre MP, Baroness Burdett-Coutts and Octavia Hill) was needed in 1884–89 to add Parliament Hill and East Park to the Heath. Golders Hill Park was purchased in 1898, Kenwood House and grounds in 1914 and then Henrietta Barnett with Thomas Barratt raised the funds to add the Heath Extension near the Hampstead Garden Suburb in 1904 (the story is well summarised in John Richardson's book *Hampstead One Thousand*).

These campaigns for the Heath gave much publicity to the subject of building development in Hampstead, and the rest of the green fields around the old village were not to survive long after Sir Thomas Maryon Wilson's death in 1869. Within the area of the village, infill building by other owners began in a few small developments in the 1850s and 1860s (for example, a row of houses at Nos. 16–28 Well Walk and another at 69–73 Heath Street). But the big building projects at that time were at the bottom of Hampstead Hill to the south, on the land belonging to Eton College (Adelaide Road and its surroundings) and to the Chapter of Westminster (around

(Opposite) 1. A map of Hampstead 1814, drawn by J. and W. Newton for J.J. Park's The Topography and Natural History of Hampstead.

2. A map of Hampstead dated 1853, showing the two Maryon-Wilson estates (shaded), still awaiting development.

what is now Belsize Village). Once Sir John Maryon Wilson had given up the battle to develop Hampstead Heath upon his elder brother's death in 1869, he started to build on the West Hampstead part of his estate (west of Finchley Road) from 1874 onwards and then along both sides of the new Fitzjohn's Avenue (which, as built in 1875–76, ran up the hill from Swiss Cottage only as far as Arkwright Road, before vanishing into a rookery of alleyways until it was cut through to join Heath Street in 1888–89).

There were strong financial incentives for Hampstead landowners to sell or develop in the 1870s and the rest of the century. Many prosperous Londoners wanted to leave the inner suburbs for the greenery, quiet and cleaner air further out. And so with changes in the legal position following the settlement with Sir John Maryon Wilson, the owners of other substantial Georgian houses in the centre of Hampstead village began to sell off or develop their grounds. Thus we find the handsome Gardnor House in Flask Walk has today only a small garden, while around it are the crammed terraces of houses along Gardnor Road, Gayton Road and Gayton Crescent (built in 1871–76) and all around Willoughby Road across to Willow Road (built in 1876–79), where once its extensive grounds fell away southwards towards the Heath.

The 1880s brought to Hampstead the more civilised architecture of the 'Queen Anne Style', the spacious red brick houses with sunflower panels and white-painted woodwork associated with the 'sweetness and light' movement, typified by Kate Greenaway's illustrations for children's books. That style developed into a freely Arts and Crafts type of design in the 1890s and, at the same time, a revival of simplified classical architecture took hold and became known as Neo-Georgian. These are the styles of most of the houses of that decade and the ensuing Edwardian period, when the big northern tract of the Maryon Wilsons' Manor Farm estate, reaching from Frognal right along Finchley Road and Redington Road to Platt's Lane, was developed with handsome middle-class homes of orange-red brick and tiles. The descriptions of these streets and buildings (and their owners at the time), that make up much of this book, are in the form of two walks that follow, as closely as is practical, the developments of houses and their architecture in and around old Hampstead village in the order they occurred.

Naturally, as the population of Hampstead grew denser in the centre and spread around it, the buildings that provided for other human needs increased too. The numbers of shops increased in established shopping centres such as the High Street and Heath Street, while new centres appeared in South End, Belsize Village and in groups at intervals along the Finchley Road. Schools, churches and banks multiplied in Hampstead, as elsewhere, during the second half of the 19th century and new amenities such as fire stations, public libraries and swimming pools appeared. To give a picture of some of these human activities, both walks described in this book include passages that tell what occupations and businesses were being pursued at each address in the main shopping streets in the 1890s and 1900s.

By the time the Great War brought the Edwardian era to a harsh close in 1914, all the green fields between Hampstead and Euston were built over. Hampstead was no longer a luxury hilltop island of fine Georgian mansions surrounding a core of slums — it had become part of London. That is the story of this book.

But the village kept much of its own character. There are still many descendants of the working class Victorians of Hampstead living in the council flats up the hill above Flask Walk and Well Walk. Many middle-class families have been there for three generations or more. The steep streets are still there, as are the alleys, courts and stone flights of steps, the glimpses of enclosed gardens, the grand Georgian houses and the handsome Victorian ones. Two designated Conservation Areas defend most of Hampstead now, yet constant vigilance is needed to stop modern equivalents of Sir Thomas Maryon Wilson from spoiling it — only last year a loophole in the law allowed a quick vulture to demolish a charming house in Fitzjohn's Avenue that seemed protected. In the High Street, shopkeepers selling food are still being driven out by new high rents, their places largely taken by boutiques and estate agents. But the wheel will turn — these new waves of trade will pass, so grocers may have their day again. As Sir Graham Jackson, whose memoirs about Hampstead began this introduction, summed up in 1905, 'Changed and vulgarised as it is, I love the old place still.' The words pre-echo the thoughts of later generations of Hampstead dwellers.

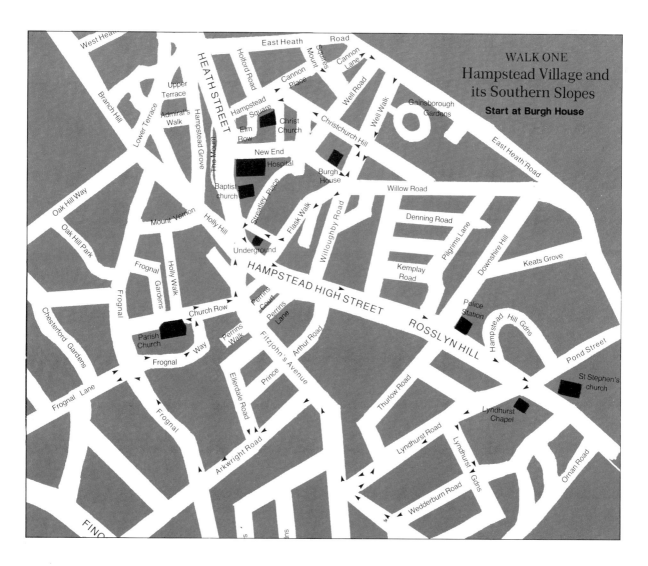

WALK ONE
Hampstead Village and
its Southern Slopes
Start at Burgh House

WALK ONE

Hampstead Village and its Southern Slopes

At the beginning of Queen Victoria's reign, Hampstead was a comparatively quiet village again after its rumbustious years as one of London's eighteenth-century spas. In 1840 it consisted of the group of buildings still to be seen in altered form around Barclays Bank and the William IV tavern in the High Street, the brick Georgian houses around Church Row, Holly Hill, Hampstead Square and Flask Walk, and ramshackle slum dwellings on the slopes between. The spa buildings in Well Walk were still there, but in disrepair or altered use. Around this central part, there were a number of quite big Georgian gentlemen's houses set in their estates of fields and orchards that spread down the steep slope to the Downshire Hill hamlet.

London, however, was well on its way northwards. As early as 1829, Cruikshank published a cartoon called *London going out of town — the March of Bricks and Mortar*, showing a hail of bricks pouring out of a kiln and falling on the hay-ricks and meadows north of the built-up streets around Fitzroy Square. A signpost on the extreme edge of the cartoon reads 'To Hampstead'. That seemed a joke in 1829.

By the 1880s, London had reached Hampstead and throughout that decade the fields around the old village were a giant muddy redevelopment area. Most of those big Georgian gentlemen's houses are still there — Foley House, Gardnor House, South Lodge, Cannon Hall, Burgh House, Squire's Mount and so on — but well before the end of the nineteenth century their rural estates had become streets of brick houses. It is that transformation of Hampstead between about 1870 and the early 1900s that this first walk, lasting a little over two hours, will trace, noting the changes in people, architectural styles and fashions as we progress.

Hampstead today is a community that mixes working classes with writers, academics with prosperous professionals, politicians with actors and musicians. Walking down the High Street from Hampstead Underground Station, and turning left between the shops and then the pretty houses of Flask Walk, we pass close to the homes of all that range of people. And it was a similar mixture in late Victorian times. The grandparents of many of the Hampstead people now living in the Council flats, then dwelt in the little cottages or charitable tenements around here. And numerous artists, writers and architects inhabited the more spacious houses that were rising in the fields around.

This first walk through Victorian Hampstead starts a short distance from Hampstead Underground Station, at Burgh House, built in 1704, one of the best of the mansion houses of wealthy families of the very early eighteenth century. This building is on the uphill corner where Flask Walk becomes Well Walk — the house itself is now a Hampstead centre for the arts and a local museum. Throughout the first half of Queen Victoria's reign, Burgh House was the headquarters of the Hampstead Militia, and the troops lived in barracks, one block spreading over the present garden below

3. Christ Church, Hampstead Square, built by Samuel Daukes 1850–52. A landmark spire to be seen from the Heath.

the house and another on the south side of Well Walk. Further along Well Walk to the east can be seen the houses numbered 16–28 in the brick Classical manner typical of early Victorian villas and the Wells Hotel, built in 1849 on the site of the Green Man, where John Keats drank with his friends. The first part of our walk will take us on a time journey through the successive stages and fashions of Victorian architecture to give a background for the rest of the buildings we shall see.

Turning left up Christchurch Hill there are stern brick houses of 1878 on the right, then typical Hampstead working class dwellings on the left. Above those, there is the Church of England Primary School (by W. AND E. HABERSHON 1854), and we reach Christ Church, which faces onto Hampstead Square.

HAMPSTEAD SQUARE

By the late 1840s, the population of Hampstead was too large for the old church in Church Row and the parish was sub-divided. **Christ Church** was designed in 1850 by an architect called SAMUEL W. DAUKES (1811–80) and completed in 1852, on the site of the old Victoria Tea Gardens. This was the year of the death of the great initiator of the Victorian Gothic Revival, Augustus Welby Pugin (designer of all the detailing and splendid interiors of the Houses of Parliament). Pugin and his many followers, especially the Ecclesiologist clergymen of the Cambridge Camden Society, succeeded in convincing most influential people in early Victorian England that the Gothic style — with its lofty proportions, soaring spires and pointed arches — was the only architecture fit for a Christian country. Daukes was a prosperous if not a major figure among the many Victorian Gothic architects. During the years he was building this church, he was also at work on St Saviour's at Tetbury in Gloucestershire, a country house called Horsted Place in Sussex, the Royal Agricultural College at Cirencester, the vast Colney Hatch lunatic asylum now called Friern Barnet Hospital, and some railway stations. His Christ Church, Hampstead is in the Early English form of Gothic, with a pleasant interior of no special distinction, but has a spire whose floodlit arrowhead floats gorgeously above many Hampstead streets at night.

Over the years, various additions were made to Christ Church by more eminent architects than its original designer. SIR GILBERT SCOTT (architect of the Albert Memorial and the grand Gothic hotel that forms the frontage of St Pancras Station), who was the most successful of all Victorian Gothic architects in terms of the amount he built, lived at Admiral's House in Admiral's Walk on the other side of Heath Street and was a member of the Christ Church congregation. He built a notable timber gallery for this church in 1860 when the congregation outgrew the seating, but this creaked ominously by the 1960s and, sadly, was pulled down. His son, GEORGE GILBERT SCOTT junior, lived in Church Row and made designs for a porch and an extra aisle for Christ Church. But these plans were rejected, and the present porch and projecting aisle were done in 1881–82 by another distinguished parishioner, EWAN CHRISTIAN, whose own house we shall see further on. (Other good examples of mid-Victorian Gothic in Hampstead include the Heath Street Baptist Chapel of 1860–61 near New End Hospital; the Rosslyn Hill Unitarian Chapel *c*1870; the former Fire Station of 1873 — now a building society office — by George Vulliamy of the Metropolitan Board of Works, on the corner of Holly Bush Hill and upper Heath Street; St Stephen's church, Rosslyn Hill, of 1869 by S.S. Teulon; and the house of Alfred Bell, the pre-eminent stained-glass maker, of 1864–65 by John Burlison, now Nos. 1 and 3 Lyndhurst Terrace.)

CANNON PLACE

Our walk now takes us from Christ Church and Hampstead Square eastwards along Cannon Place into the most tranquil lanes of Hampstead village. At the end of Cannon Place, (note the blue plaque on one of the row of quite small Victorian villas on the left — built 1875–77 by William Shepherd — recording that Sir Flinders Petrie, the great Egyptologist and archaeologist, lived there), we come to two of Hampstead's large Georgian houses, both dating from *c*1720 though no architects' names are known. **Cannon Hall**, on the right, was extensively altered in 1885 for its owner James Marshall, and the Classical entrance addition dates from *c*1900. Opposite this, the

4. The Logs at the corner of East Heath Road and Well Road, Edward Gotto's fantastic house.

artist Walter Stacey lived at No. 1 Cannon Place in the 1890s. **Squire's Mount**, a long Georgian block with its end towards the road, was the home of the wealthy Field family in Victorian times. One of that family, HORACE FIELD (1861–1948), became a successful architect. He was the designer of many buildings in Hampstead and was later more widely important in the introduction of the Neo-Georgian style. Field was a pupil of Sir John Burnet in Glasgow, then of R.W. Edis in London, and started his own practice in 1882. He lived in the part of Squire's Mount nearest the road (the house was called Chestnut Lodge at that time) and the *c*1900 extension of the house towards the entrance gate was presumably his design. His central London work includes the *Church Times* building near the Law Courts and Neo-Georgian houses and offices in the streets south of Westminster Abbey, while further afield he built the splendid headquarters of the London and North-Eastern Railway in York. We shall see many pretty designs by him later on this Hampstead walk.

WELL ROAD

We now go down the hill by the narrow, almost rustic, Cannon Lane and turn left along Well Road. At the end of this, on the corner with East Heath Road and overlooking Hampstead Heath, stands Hampstead's fantasy monster, Edward Gotto's house **The Logs**. Gotto was a successful civil engineer and developer of the land in this part of Hampstead. When he became rich, he built his own house in 1868, adding wings to each side of it eight years later. The old main gateway now has 'Lion House' written above it, but it was built as 'The Logs', and the central part is still called that. The named architect was J.S. NIGHTINGALE, of whom nothing else is known (though there is a story that he built an aquarium in Brighton), and it seems that Gotto himself was perhaps largely responsible for the design. Indeed, few trained architects would have combined Gothic, Italianate and other styles into an overall design of such ogrish panache, with towers, spires and gargoyles galore. The huge house is now subdivided — the central part (which has a splendid oval Victorian staircase up into the gargan-

5. *The Pryors, East Heath Road. These blocks, overlooking the Vale of Health, are on the site of an earlier encroachment on the Heath.*

tuan tower) is unpredictable in a way worthy of its owner in the 1970s, the late comedian Marty Feldman, and has so far been well cared for by his successors. Is The Logs ugly? Undoubtedly. But it has imagination, character and a grotesque Victorian splendour to it, all the same.

EAST HEATH ROAD

We turn down East Heath Road, dodging the speeding traffic, past the Georgian Foley House (Gotto bought it as an investment and added the porch in 1880), notice the two large blocks of flats called **The Pryors** (by HART AND WATERHOUSE, 1910 and *c*1920) on the Heath side of the road, and turn right into Well Walk. There, at No. 50 Well Walk astride the corner, is one of the best Victorian houses in Hampstead — **Thwaitehead** (now called **Klippar House**) built in 1881–82 by the architect EWAN CHRISTIAN, for himself. Christian (1814–95) was an important if second-rank architect of the Gothic revival, a contemporary of Sir Gilbert Scott and William Butterfield. He built a number of good Victorian Gothic churches and added chancels and other extensions to countless old churches around England. He became Architectural Advisor to the Church Commissioners, President of the RIBA and winner of its Royal Gold Medal in 1887. His largest building was his last, the National Portrait Gallery, built surprisingly in an Italianate style in 1890–95.

Ewan Christian was indeed an artist, and a very pious one. His house reflects these qualities, for it is a subtle design — the volumes and the complex roofs play with each other as one moves around it, and there is much lovely metalwork on the exterior. The enormous wrought-iron lamp bracket was made in Nuremburg in *c*1600, and bought by Christian for his house when he was travelling in Germany. The building has a broad band around its wall which was originally inscribed with biblical texts. A curious story is attached to this house — it seems that Christian, as Advisor to the Church Commissioners, rejected some designs by the talented George Gilbert Scott junior, perhaps those for Christ Church up the hill. Scott was often mentally disturbed in his later years, and when he heard this news he came over from his house in Church Row, summoned Christian to his own front door and urinated on the doorstep to

(Above) 6. Klippar House, East Heath Road, home of the Victorian architect Ewan Christian. One of the best Victorian houses in Hampstead.

(Opposite page, top) 7. Postcard, c1906 showing Well Walk and the drinking fountain.

(Opposite page, bottom) 8. The first Long Room in Well Walk, painted by J.P. Emslie in 1879, shortly before its demolition. Gainsborough Gardens was built over its grounds.

show his disgust. Such human dramas cannot detract from the artistic excellence of Christian's design, even in its current dilapidated state.

Down the hill from Ewan Christian's house, there are two houses built by him as investments in the 1880s and, on the opposite side of East Heath Road, the earlier block of The Pryors flats. These are reminders of the seemingly engulfing greed of developers in Hampstead in the 1880s and the heroic campaign that saved Hampstead Heath from them during that decade.

WELL WALK

Walking along Well Walk, we pass a rather dashing terrace of houses on the right (Nos. 21–27) of 1881, developed by Edward Gotto and designed by HENRY LEGG and approach the part of Hampstead where, in the 1870s, the old Spa buildings still survived. The sole reminder of it now is the stone fountain (1882) on the north side of the road. Sadly, it yields only London mains water today, rather than the mineral well water that made Georgian Hampstead fashionable. Opposite the well is the site of the original Spa building, across the entrance of what is now Gainsborough Gardens. The building and its large entertainment garden were redeveloped completely during the 1880s, and provide us with an example of the new Victorian architectural style of that time.

At the start of this walk we noticed the quietly Classical villas of grey brick with white-painted artificial sculpted stone further along Well Walk at Nos. 16–28, and the pointed Gothic arches of Christ Church, both typical styles of the early Victorian period. Now it is time to talk of later Victorian architecture — the so-called Queen Anne style and the new sort of house design that became fashionable from 1870

onwards. The trademarks of the 'Queen Anne' style are cheerful red brick, white-painted woodwork and white moulded plasterwork, with tall windows and other more or less Classical details used very freely in a way said to be derived from the typical English domestic work of around 1700 (whence 'Queen Anne'). External wall decoration by terracotta panels of sunflowers are a key motif. Buildings in this style often had Flemish touches and even some traces of Gothic thrown in to make up recipes that varied with each house designed. One common variant was the sort of tile-hanging as an external surface of the upper walls that is a traditional feature of houses in the Weald of southern England. The new architecture was part of a wider change in the life style of the upper middle classes in the 1870s, a way of life caught by the phrase 'Sweetness and Light'. Pretty gardens, charming children's clothes of the sort seen in books illustrated by Kate Greenaway, light and spacious rooms — all of these were part of the new fashion. The architects who introduced and popularised variations of the Queen Anne style from 1870 onwards were J.J. STEVENSON (1831–1908), PHILIP WEBB (1831–1915), W. EDEN NESFIELD (1835–1888), most especially R. NORMAN SHAW (1831–1912) and a number of Shaw's followers. Of these, Stevenson is represented in Hampstead by the unworthily ponderous No. 1 Fitzjohn's Avenue (1883), Philip Webb — ally of William Morris and idol of the Socialist young Arts and Crafts architects of the 1890s — by the prettily tile-hung Nos. 2 and 4 Redington Road (1876, described in the second of these walks), Nesfield not at all and Shaw the maestro by three major houses described later. The Queen Anne style reached Hampstead in 1875 in Norman Shaw's design for his own house (which we shall see later), and most of the domestic buildings of the 1880s and early 1890s are in this manner.

GAINSBOROUGH GARDENS

In **Gainsborough Gardens**, off Well Walk, we meet the influence of these innovators in all its variety, as carried out by their followers. The entrance had been the site of the first Long Room of the Spa, which became a chapel and then, by the 1870s, a drill hall. Behind the Long Room was a pleasure garden with a pond and sculptured fountain. A plan to build a grid of streets across this was defeated in 1879 and the development was carried out during the 1880s around the pleasure garden, which is still there in altered form, though the pond has vanished. No. 1 (Wellside) is handsome and dates from 1892, architect unknown. The excellent Nos. 3 and 4 (1883) are by E.J. MAY, a Norman Shaw pupil who did much work at Bedford Park and used the tile-hung manner with lots of personal idiosyncracies. Walking clockwise around the central garden, Nos. 6, 7, 8, 9, 9a, 10 and the tiny gardener's cottage (like a lodge at the entrance) are all 1884–86 designs by HENRY LEGG, and display many of the Queen Anne style characteristics already described, done with a talent that varies from the acceptable to the inadequate — notice the panels of tiles showing sunflowers and other 'sweetness and light' motifs.

   At one side of this oval of houses around the gardens lies No. 14 (The Small House) of 1891 by HORACE FIELD (of Squire's Mount, mentioned above) in a style between the Queen Anne and the Neo-Georgian, for his mother Mrs Horace Field. Nos. 11–13 are also by Field, but of 1893, in a fully 'Neo-Georgian' manner and very early for that style. From that time on, this adaptation of the English Classical architecture of the Georgian period was increasingly important, as we shall see, and became the dominant style for middle-class houses built after 1900 in the Edwardian period.

WELL WALK continued

Completing the tour around Gainsborough Gardens, we go on along Well Walk past Nos. 32–46 (which are Georgian, with porches added around 1900) and on the north side Nos. 15–17 of 1884 and 11–13 of 1879, past the Wells Hotel and then Nos. 16–28 already mentioned. Here, on the north side of Well Walk is the Wells House estate of

ainsborough Gardens,

WELL WALK, HAMPSTEAD HEATH.

Ebor House *occupies, in owner's opinion, the
nd-best site, being on the elevated part with
hern frontage and with shelter from north and
winds. It has no contact with heath or public
l and is therefore free from occasional disadvan-
s, is a place of quiet without gloom, in the midst
old trees and bird-life, and, as the principal
ns are on the first floor with spacious well lit
l and staircase between, it is a most desirable
dence for those who want the wonderful good
ch results from full enjoyment of strong light
air. A person of weak health might perhaps be
ed to quite new life, for sunshine is more than ever
eved to be a powerful enemy to many forms of
ase. Writer is justified in his remarks by
rience in his own family next door. The house
unusually well built and fitted, and the interior
some little distinction.*

*Reduced rent, on lease, £145, and 4 guineas
cription to grounds; or sale by private treaty.
thirds of purchase money could remain on
gage at 4½ per cent.*

flats (by C.H. JAMES, built 1949–51) on the site of the Spa's second Long Room and Assembly Room of c1740, which had been converted into a Tudorish house during the 1870s. So we return to the front of Burgh House, where we started this walk. From what we have seen so far, we can look at the intense development of the rest of upper hillside Hampstead with an understanding of the historical sequence and the main architectural styles involved. We have seen examples of early Victorian Classicism and Gothic style, mid-Victorian eclecticism mixing various styles, later Gothicism, the Queen Anne manner of the 1880s with its varieties later, and the Neo-Georgian revived in the 1890s onwards. There remain to be seen the two other main Edwardian styles — the florid Baroque Classicism fashionable for large buildings around 1900, and the simple bold designs of the Arts and Crafts movement architects.

9. An undated sale advertisement for a house in Gainsborough Gardens.

10. Weatherall House, Well Walk, the second Long Room. Drawing by Quinton 1911.

FLASK WALK

In 1880–82 the barracks in front of Burgh House and on the other side of the road were demolished and Nos. 2–14 Well Walk were put up by a builder called George Price in a cheap but pleasant version of the Queen Anne style. This was the period when most of the owners of the large Georgian houses in Hampstead sold their land to developers and the Heath was under threat. Moving across Willow Road and along Flask Walk, we pass on the right No. 75 (Rosemount) with its tall Regency elegance of 1813, in which the poet Alfred Lord Tennyson (1809–92) spent much of his heyday in his sister's house when visiting London, and on the left a studded gateway brought from George Dance's Newgate Gaol of 1770 when it was demolished in 1902. We stop on the

11. Gardnor House by
J.P. Emslie in 1879.

green triangle opposite Gardnor House. **Gardnor House**, across the street down the hill, was a solitary Georgian mansion in its own grounds until 1869, when legal restrictions on its land were ended and the rise in land prices of the 1860s brought an immediate sale. Here we see a microcosm of what happened to most of Hampstead in the following decades. The grounds of Gardnor House stretched from the present Willow Road to Hampstead High Street and well down the hill. After the land was sold, the houses in the dead-end Gardnor Road, of impoverished inspiration, went up in 1871–72, while Gayton Road and Gayton Crescent followed later in the 1870s. Finally, the houses of upper Willow Road, Willoughby Road and its offshoots were started around 1876, and Gardnor House was left with only the present-day sliver of garden to inspire its later owners, including the novelists Kingsley Amis and Elizabeth Jane Howard, who had it in the 1970s.

Standing on the Flask Walk green, we can also look uphill and see signs of why Hampstead is the mixed-class community it is today. The Georgian houses belong to actors, writers, poets and the like, but above these we can see the now threatened working-class dwellings of **New Court** (the larger block 1854, the smaller 1871, both the idea of solicitor Hugh Jackson, father of Sir T.G. Jackson the noted architect who rebuilt much of Hampstead Parish Church); the splendid **New End Schools** (T.J. BAILEY and the LCC schools architects, 1903, in a Baroque manner of truly Edwardian flamboyance) and, in Flask Walk itself, the muscular Wells and Campden Baths and Wash-house (as inscribed on charitable red brick), designed by HENRY LEGG, 1888. For ninety years, this building provided austerely hygienic baths for the people in the bath-less working-class tenements up the hill — an odd successor to the fashionable Spa buildings along the road — before conversion into private houses in 1981.

FLASK WALK SHOPS

Walking past the trim Georgian houses along Flask Walk, we reach the point where the already narrow street becomes no more than a pedestrian passage lined by shops.

In late Victorian times, and later, this lane was open to horse-drawn and other traffic, leaving only a tightrope of pavement between the carts and carriages and the shop fronts. In the 1890s the shops and tradesmen's premises spread further along Flask Walk than now. East of Back Lane, there were ten places of work. Nos. 20 to 36 were private houses but on that side there was also a group Nos. 38–40 including a bootmaker, a laundry, a zincographer and two carpenters. On the other side of the road were three dressmakers, a builder and at No. 29 lived Elvy Cork, a gardener.

Farther along, in the narrowest part of Flask Walk where it runs through into the High Street, there was almost a complete village shopping centre in miniature. On the left as we walk in this direction, is the famous Flask Tavern, a warmly hospitable public house that still has much of its original architecture (1873–74) outside and in the bars. Beyond this, we have to imagine a crowded dozen or more Victorian shops on either side. There were in 1894 two butchers (one of them selling pork only), two bakers, two fishmongers, a grocer, a greengrocer, at No. 4 Stefani the Italian ice-cream maker, two hairdressers, a tailor, a bootmaker, an oilman, a leather seller, a tobacconist and at No. 6 the West End Dining Rooms.

The route of our walk turns right just before we reach the Flask Tavern, up another narrow street, Back Lane, which is lined by little Victorian working-class cottages now much prettified.

HEATH STREET
Back Lane rises steeply and joins Heath Street, one of Hampstead's main traffic arteries that remains narrow and picturesque. We turn left down the slope of Heath

12. New End Schools, off Flask Walk. Detail of a Baroque classroom tower, designed by T.J. Bailey, the London County Council's head schools architect and his staff (1903).

13. The Horse and Groom, Heath Street. Product of the pub boom of the 1890s, its fine Arts and Crafts frontage of c1897 is attributed to Treadwell and Martin, architects of such well-known pubs of the time as the Old Shades in Whitehall and the Rising Sun in Tottenham Court Road.

Street for a few yards and pause on the platform in front of the **Kingswell Shopping Centre**, built in 1967 to the designs of the late TED LEVY, a well-known local architect. From the viewpoint of this platform we can see down Heath Street to its junction with the High Street and Holly Hill, and up Heath Street as it winds higher towards Hampstead Heath. Thirty yards up the hill rises the **Horse and Groom** public house, a splendid example of late Victorian pub architecture. It is a brilliant towering composition of chequered Portland stone and red brick. Slender piers rise all the way from the ground to the flamboyant gable, passing bow windows and some good sculpture.

The Horse and Groom dates from c1897 and was probably designed by TREADWELL AND MARTIN (who built countless pubs and office buildings in central London at the time in an Arts and Crafts manner derived from the Gothic, such as the Old Shades in Whitehall and the Rising Sun in Tottenham Court Road). There was a boom in public house building in the 1890s when a new lower middle class of underpaid clerks walked home from inner London to the suburbs every evening, and the pedestrian crowds could be attracted from the darkness of the streets for most of the year to the

14. The old Fire Station at the corner of High Street and Heath Street, built in 1873.

light and cheer of increasingly ambitious pubs. Landlords competed with each other in rebuilding, and 84 new public house building tenders were invited in London in 1898. Then came a crash. Over-extended publicans went bankrupt by scores. In 1900 only eight pub tenders were invited, and the ruined businesses were picked up — 314 of them by 1903 — by an 'Improved Public House' charity (women, food and soft drinks were encouraged) that later became Trust House Forte.

Down the hill from the Kingswell Shopping Centre, beyond the traffic lights, the Heath Street extension was cut through slum cottages in 1886–88 to join up with Fitzjohn's Avenue. At the traffic lights, on the right of the street, there stands the Gothic style **Fire Station** (of 1873, by GEORGE VULLIAMY, head of the Metropolitan Board of Works' Architects' Department, now a building society office). Originally the large fire engines kept there were pulled by fast horses. I never saw the horses, but as a child in the late 1930s I remember watching the clanging red monsters swooping out of here across the traffic to spray some Hampstead fire.

15. Hampstead Underground Station. Designed 1906–07 by Leslie Green, the architect to the Underground Electric Railways. Modernisation has recently taken place and many features have been lost.

HAMPSTEAD UNDERGROUND STATION

Walking down Heath Street, we come to the **Hampstead Underground Station**, one of the earliest in London and still the deepest. It was built in 1906–07, designed by the architect of Underground Electric Railways Ltd, LESLIE GREEN — whose Classical ox-blood tiled stations are familiar in many parts of London. The story behind the public transport of the early Edwardian period is extraordinary. At first the electric trams came to the edge of central London in the 1890s, with the tube trains connecting to the tram terminals across the middle. The first tube, the Central Line from Mansion House in the City to Shepherd's Bush, opened in July 1900. The Northern, Piccadilly and Bakerloo lines' inner sections followed within a few years — all of them the inspiration of a truly indomitable American engineer-entrepreneur called Charles T. Yerkes. When the Northern Line opened to Hampstead and Golders Green in 1907, adventurous estate agents started business in huts on the fields beyond Hampstead hill. Thus the possibility of commuting to the suburbs opened up for the new generation of clerks, and the *rus in urbe* dream of Hampstead Garden Suburb started to become a reality. Today, with the grimy delays of the Northern Line, it is hard to appreciate the miracle of the Underground. And so, few people notice the elegance of the *Art Nouveau* detailing around the older lifts of Hampstead Station; sadly that around the ticket offices has recently been removed. It is to be hoped that all this will be retained and enhanced by the 'refurbishment' proposals for the station put forward by London Regional Transport in the late 1980s.

16. The site of Hampstead Underground Station. To the extreme left of the picture may be seen the two street name plates at the corner of Heath Street and High Street.

HAMPSTEAD HIGH STREET

Going down the High Street below the tube station, this walk passes a succession of good Victorian buildings, as well as the surviving Georgian houses of the older village core on both sides between Oriel Place and Prince Arthur Road. Between Nos. 30 and 35, on the left going down the hill, there is a large development of 1984–86 with shops in front and mews-style houses behind. Most of the other buildings were existing in about 1890, though with very different shops at ground level from the women's clothes boutiques, estate agents, cafés, supermarkets, opticians and building societies that predominate around a century later. It is illuminating to get a mental picture of the High Street in the last decade of Queen Victoria's reign from the street directories of the time.

On the side of the High Street running down the hill opposite the tube station and the end of Flask Walk, there is a large building put up as a commercial development in 1887–89, replacing a warren of alleys and courts. The frontage of the buildings is made up of a succession of gabled designs — notice that there are only three designs, though they are put together in various combinations. The style is a commercial form of the Queen Anne manner fashionable in the 1880s, which appears repeatedly in fine as well as versions throughout this walk. In the early 1890s the top corner shop in this block was T.J. Lipton, the celebrated tea merchant, and on the floors above, the costumiers A. and J. Girling. Next down the hill was the shop of Lilley and Skinner, bootmakers then as now. Then at No. 57 was Harrington's the confectioner, with Mrs. Dunkley, medical rubber, in the floors above. At No. 59 was a bicycle works, A.J. Selley and Co., then Mrs Tindley's ham and beef warehouse, Palmer's china and glass, and the Victoria Wine Co. (the sole survivor today). At No. 63 was John Alfred Shepherd, fine art dealer, at No. 64 (on the corner of Oriel Place) the London and Commercial Meat Stores, with the Oriel Dairy behind.

On the other corner of Oriel Place and the High Street, Zwanziger Bros. sold their celebrated confectionery and pastry in the 1890s. Beside them at No. 68 was the

Hampstead agency of the Wigan Coal and Iron Company, with the harnessmaker Frederick Pearn on the upper floors. Then there was a butcher at No. 69 and in No. 70 a fine mixture of professions — Sydney Mayle sold English and foreign books, Miss Bell made dresses, Miss Earl kept a Berlin repository, and a Mrs. Courtier pursued an unnamed occupation.

On the two corners of Perrins Court, where the upper storeys of the building bridge over the opening to the lane, there were Skoyles the ironmonger and, at No. 73, the famous quality grocer Forster's (proprietor in that generation, James Forster) which closed only in the 1960s. Then followed a builder, another harnessmaker, Mrs. Sell the house agent and at No. 76 the office of The New River Company.

Beyond Church (now Perrins) Lane, the William the Fourth public house, which still survives, was already old. Next to it there was a jobmaster at No. 77, Mr Smellie the carpenter at No. 79, a bootmaker, a fruiterer and over No. 81 and behind it the celebrated local newspaper the *Hampstead and Highgate Express* whose editor then was George Jealous; this was, until recently, in Perrins Court and is now based in Finchley Road. Finally on this side of the High Street before reaching its end at Prince Arthur Road, there was Dolman's art pottery at No. 82 and at Nos. 83/4 Willis's the ironmonger, later a builder and timber merchant. But go up the slope and around the corner here into Prince Arthur Road to see the gem of a building at No. 2A on the right that was originally a small **Christian Science Reading Room**, designed by HORACE FIELD in a charming Neo-Georgian style and built in 1890–91. On the corner itself is **Stanfield House**, a Georgian building, home in the mid 19th century of the eminent seascape painter Clarkson Stanfield, and later of the celebrated Hampstead Subscription Library.

Returning to the Hampstead tube station side of the road, where the station's shiny

17. High Street and Perrins Court in the 1890s. This picture shows, from right to left, Skoyle's the ironmonger at no. 72, Forster's, the already long-established grocer at no. 73, and Hudson the builder-decorator.

walls occupy the top of the High Street, in the early 1890s there was a watchmaker at No. 50 and a chemist at No. 49 on the corner of the passage called Minerva Place. Below that was the Hampstead Branch Post Office. Then came Evans Hill and Sons, occupying two shops with their drapery business, and W.and H. King with groceries at 45 and stationery at 44. On the uphill corner of Flask Walk was Body's bakery and below it the provision dealer, Lambert. A tobacconist at No. 41 was beside another opening off the street, this one into the stables of the London General Omnibus Co. At No. 40 was an oilman and then came the Bird in Hand public house which is still going well with its mid-Victorian restrained classical building of 1878 cheered up by a ground floor of *c*1905 Edwardian glazed tiles.

Continuing downhill from the Bird in Hand, there was a series of small buildings here in Victorian times, now replaced by a large modern development. In the 1890s there was a fishmonger at No. 37, Harvey Shillingford the grocers at 36, a dressmaker, builder, and stationer all at 34, a butcher, and then the hosiers and hatters, Edwin Evans, Hill and Sons. There followed a tailor, a bootmaker called Flatau and in No. 30 Elliott and Co who sold provisions in the shop, corn at the rear and let the upper floor to Miss Chambers, a dressmaker. At No. 29 is the second shop in the High Street that is still in the same use as a century ago. This is Edward B. Stamp, who described the shop's business as 'pharmaceutical chemist' in the early 1890s. Next to Stamp's the grandly debased classical building of Barclay's Bank was that of its forerunner, the London and South-Western. At No. 28a was the Hampstead Floral Depot and usefully beside that the undertaker Clowser. Then followed a draper, an ironmonger, a tailor and, at No. 22 on the corner with Gayton Road, the house agent and auctioneer Potter's, still active in Hampstead from different premises.

Below Gayton Road, the shops were baker, boot-maker, butcher, poulterer and at Nos. 13–14 Lloyds Bank, which moved down the street in 1896 to new premises in Rosslyn Hill (see below). At Nos. 11–12, one James Hewetson traded as bookseller, binder, printer and fancy warehouseman. The King of Bohemia was backed by Hampstead Brewery. At No. 9 there was a watchmaker. The next three shop units have been, until recently, the famous High Hill Bookshop, run by Ian Norrie since the 1950s. At No. 7 Rabbits and Sons made boots and Robert Annis offered millinery and

18. Barclay's Bank, High Street. Built as the London and South-Western Bank in early Victorian times, the swanky classical frontage was added later in the 19th century.

19. Rosslyn Hill Chapel, 1911. From a drawing by A.R. Quinton.

drapery. At No. 6 Mr. Chant's business was in hardware, decoration and trunks, while Frederick Poole did upholstery at 6a. Next door, Arrowsmith Brothers were pianoforte manufacturers at Nos. 4 and 5, while Pearse's bakery was at 3. Finally and uncomfortably, Brewers Yard opened here to give access to the back of the brewery while the teetotallers of the Trinity Presbyterian Church, including my grandparents newly-arrived from Scotland in the 1890s, attended divine service in the church (bombed in 1941) next door on the corner of Willoughby Road.

ROSSLYN HILL

Below Willoughby Road and the green opposite, if we cross to the right hand side of the road (which becomes Rosslyn Hill here) we can enjoy the ambitious gabled row of buildings opposite, with 'E D', 'J B' and 'Dudman's Stores' written large in the terracotta of 1890. The **Rosslyn Hill Unitarian Chapel** (in the Victorian Gothic style by JOHN JOHNSON, 1862, extended 1885, north aisle, chancel and committee room by THOMAS WORTHINGTON, a Manchester Unitarian), is set back from the street in a garden. But the Rosslyn Arms pub (1869) and the next important building, Lloyds Bank, abut on the road.

Lloyds Bank, Rosslyn Hill, is one of the best buildings in Hampstead and one of the most attractive of its period in London. It is also one of the two or three *chef d'oeuvres* of the late Victorian Hampstead architect, HORACE FIELD, whose works play such a decorative part in this walk. The building dates from 1895–96, and is in an early and delicate version of the Edwardian Baroque style that was to dominate English public buildings for the following fifteen years.

The Baroque architecture, intentionally a very English form, of the late Victorian and Edwardian period had its roots in the increasing nationalism of the British people from the 1880s onwards. In 1889 John Brydon (architect of the Chelsea Town Hall of 1887, and later of the vast Government Offices on Parliament Square and many public buildings in Bath) gave a lecture to the Architectural Association in praise of Wren, Hawksmoor and Vanbrugh as creators of a truly *English* Classical style — a style fit for

20. Lloyd's Bank,
Rosslyn Hill, built 1895-6.
Designed by Horace
Field in a style that later
became known as
Edwardian Baroque.

the modern capital of the world's greatest empire. His ideas were put into practice by the pre-eminent architect of the time, Norman Shaw, and many others. Horace Field was one of these and what he did in the Edwardian Baroque style or in its quieter Neo-Georgian domestic equivalent, was done finely and done early in the style's development.

In the Lloyds Bank building, Field took a rather difficult corner site and erected a building in soft brick with elegant stone trimming. The lower windows have big round arches of rusticated stone, while the upper ones are charmingly shuttered. It is irresistible in the love and inventiveness evidently poured into its design.

Going on down Rosslyn Hill we come to another striking architectural work of the turn of the century. This is the **Hampstead Police Station** of 1910–13, with its Magistrates' Court around the corner in Downshire Hill. The Metropolitan Police Force was enlarged considerably at the turn of the century, and London has many police stations of that time. The designer of most of them was J. DIXON BUTLER, architect to the Metropolitan Police, and his bold manner is easy to recognise. Butler had worked for Norman Shaw on the New Scotland Yard headquarters, and that influence lingered. Basically, Butler's usual style was Baroque. But he had a way of sweeping his roofs up into powerful gables, and of using very strong and simple Classical detailing for his doorways and windows. That strength shows the influence on Butler's designs of the Arts and Crafts architects then working for the London County Council on its fine housing estates and fire stations of that time (e.g. in Hampstead, the fire stations in West End Lane of 1901 and in Eton Avenue of 1914–15). The Hampstead Police Station is typical of Dixon Butler and, with its massive front gable of brick and its punchy stone Baroque detailing, is one of his best works.

Further down Rosslyn Hill we pass a pretty pair of tile-hung houses on the right (Nos. 17–29 of the 1880s). These show one kind of influence of Norman Shaw, while the houses on the left along the quiet side road here, **Hampstead Hill Gardens**, show other aspects of the Queen Anne style: Nos. 1–9 on one side and Nos. 2 and 4 on the other, plus No. 12 Rosslyn Hill on the corner, all apparently designed by BATTERBURY AND HUXLEY between 1875 and 1881. No. 9 was built for the excellent watercolour painter Thomas Collier.

21. Hampstead Police Station, Rosslyn Hill. Detail of the Arts and Crafts free Baroque building of 1910–13, designed by J. Dixon Butler, a Norman Shaw pupil, who became architect to the Metropolitan Police.

22. St. Stephen's church, Haverstock Hill. This massive building by S.S. Teulon is now empty and the subject of many planning proposals.

THE GREAT VICTORIAN CHURCHES

Down Rosslyn Hill again we reach two of Hampstead's major Victorian monuments, both by nationally well-known architects. On the left at the top of Pond Street is **St Stephen's Church** of 1869–71, by S.S. TEULON (1812–73), a major Victorian architect

who lived just down the hill. This, as with so many of Teulon's churches, is mid-Victorian Gothic at its most thunderous. Beyond a wrought-iron entrance gate of exceptional delicacy, the great bulk of the church rises in dark purple brick with stone dressings. There are strong buttresses and a great wheel window as the forms mount up towards the massive tower with its steep pyramidal roof that is so familiar in the distance to anyone who walks on Hampstead Heath. Strongly buttressed, yes — but not strongly enough. I have known the church and its gloriously mysterious interior since childhood, for my grandfather retired as an Archdeacon from his missionary life to spend his last pastoral years at St Stephen's. Even then there were rumours of it slipping down the hill and cracking. This movement was accelerated when the foundations for the Royal Free Hospital were started and, although it has now stopped, the church authorities seem bent on demolishing this *pièce de résistance* of fierce Victorian extremism — described by Ruskin as 'the finest specimen of brick building in all the land.'

23. Alfred Waterhouse (1830–1905), whose most famous works included the Natural History Museum and the Prudential Building.

St Stephen's was originally an offspring of the Georgian church of St John's, Downshire Hill, built to provide for the growing Victorian congregation. The land, at the top of the pretty Hampstead Green, was donated by the lord of the manor, Sir Thomas Maryon Wilson, as early as 1864, and most of the building cost was collected in five or ten pound amounts from the parishioners. The commission to design it was first offered to Ewan Christian (whose house we have seen on this walk), who 'graciously declined' for unstated reasons, then to Teulon — already a noted Low Church architect. Teulon insisted on brick inside and out — the dark exterior contrasting with panels and bands of pale yellow, white and grey brick inside (though London grime has darkened that too). The eventual cost of £27,000 was three times the estimate, for extra funds were poured into fine carving and stained-glass windows, most of them still surviving as one hopes the church itself will.

If St Stephen's is splendidly ferocious, the **Congregational Church** of 1883–84 on the opposite side of Rosslyn Hill is downright grim. It is the work of ALFRED WATER-HOUSE, the tough northern architect of Manchester Town Hall and of London's Natural History Museum. Again it is of dark purple brick, but the pointed arches of

24. Lyndhurst Road Chapel, a postcard c1906.

*25. The Hoo, 17
Lyndhurst Gardens.
Detail of one of Horace
Field's very best designs
still, at this time (1889),
working in his charming
version of the Queen
Anne style's tile-hung
variant.*

Teulon's Victorian Gothic are here replaced by round arches of a Romanesque or Norman kind. The narrow yard at its side is worth experiencing. The church inside is hexagonal, its hard surfaces (so typical of Waterhouse) nowadays painted in pastels in an effort to ingratiate it with a modern congregation. But this church too is under threat of demolition, so we are in danger of losing both of these two stern Victorian sentries at the approach to Hampstead village.

LYNDHURST ROAD AND LYNDHURST GARDENS

Going up Lyndhurst Road, at the side of Waterhouse's church, we pass a pretty Regency villa called Rosslyn Lodge and then a row of Gothic houses of the 1870s on the left. At No. 5 the architect A.W.S. Cross, designer of the Hampstead Liberal Club in Heath Street and many schools and swimming baths (including the old Hampstead Baths in Finchley Road) lived at the end of the century. Beyond these, we are in HORACE FIELD territory again. Field began as very much a Queen Anne style and Norman Shaw disciple. At Nos. 19–21 Lyndhurst Road (1897–98), with their shared garden, we see a restrained variation of Field's other distinguished and pretty Neo-Georgian buildings that we have already enjoyed on this walk. But walking down Lyndhurst Gardens beside these Neo-Georgian houses, we soon come to No. 17 on the right, **The Hoo**, a really splendid earlier house of 1889 designed by Field for Russell Scott. This was built before the architect turned to the Neo-Georgian Classical manner. The architectural forms are fine and strong, and the tile-hanging, so typical of this version of the Queen Anne style, adds pleasure without detracting from that strength. Both the earlier part and the extension towards the road are by Field, and even the modern fire escapes cannot disguise the fact that this is one of the best pieces of architecture in Hampstead.

WEDDERBURN ROAD

A little further down Lyndhurst Gardens, we turn right into the quiet Wedderburn Road. On the north side are moderate semi-detached houses of 1896 by W.A. BURR (see also Bracknell Gardens on our second walk). Opposite them, on the south or left-hand side on this walk, all the buildings are early works by HORACE FIELD and they include

some excellent designs. First comes a block of flats called **Wedderburn House**, built 1884–85 in a stern style derived from Norman Shaw and with some odd details. This mansion block was perhaps the first of its kind in Hampstead and was originally partly inhabited by the architect's maiden aunts. Nos. 3 and 5 Wedderburn Road are of *c*1886, set back from the road, both pretty designs and No. 5 one of Field's best works. Nos. 7 and 9 date from *c*1890, quiet and pleasant designs, though the relationship of door to bow window is clumsy. Nos. 11 and 13 were perhaps the first houses of this series, the earliest of Field's speculative ventures — they date from about 1883 and are much fussier than the other designs. Last of the row is No. 15, ruined by crass rebuilding and plate-glass windows.

LYNDHURST TERRACE

That brings the walk to Akenside Road, where we turn right up the hill past some nice houses of the 1890s, until we reach the end of Lyndhurst Road on the right, and turn along it for thirty yards to see one of the most notable buildings in Hampstead, and its first Victorian Gothic house. This is Alfred Bell's house, on the corner of Lyndhurst Terrace and now numbered **1 and 3** in that street. The house was built in 1864–65 to the designs of JOHN BURLISON (Sir Gilbert Scott's chief assistant) aided by Bell himself, who was one of the pre-eminent makers of Victorian stained glass. The products of his firm, Clayton and Bell, can be seen in many houses and countless churches around England — we shall see numerous good and some poor examples in Hampstead Parish Church (where Bell was a devoted parishioner) at the end of this walk. Andrew Saint has traced the history of this house. Burlison was Bell's father-in-law and, as first built, the house contained residences for both families with an internal door between. But Burlison died in 1868 and Alfred Bell's family took over the whole building and called it Bayford House. Bell then employed another Gilbert Scott pupil, CHARLES

26. 1 and 3 Lyndhurst Terrace. Alfred Bell's house on the corner of Lyndhurst Road, built by John Burlison and Bell 1864–65.

27. Hampstead Tower (formerly Fitzjohn Tower), Fitzjohn's Avenue, built in 1881 by J.T. Wimperis. (See following page.)

BUCKERIDGE, and the two men produced a Gothic interior as wild and ornamented as any. After Bell's death in 1895, when his combined Bayford House was divided into two again, most of this memorable interior was gradually destroyed. But the brick exterior — with its many Gothic windows, round *tourettes* and big roofs — gives some flavour of what the house must have been, and inside No. 1 there are still some of the original details and one of Bell's stained-glass windows.

FITZJOHN'S AVENUE

Now we retrace our steps to Akenside Road and, turning right, arrive at once in Fitzjohn's Avenue. This was a major road cut through the green fields of Hampstead hillside and opened by Prince Arthur of Connaught in 1876. The long avenue provided a route from the early Victorian white stucco villas around Swiss Cottage and the main Finchley Road, up between meadows full of grazing cattle to old Hampstead village at the top of the hill. The cows were soon robbed of their pasture, for the development of houses started along Fitzjohn's Avenue at once. J.J. STEVENSON (No. 1 of 1883) and NORMAN SHAW built houses at the lower end, but Shaw's was demolished in the 1950s. Almost opposite the point where this walk enters Fitzjohn's Avenue, No. 55 offers an enjoyable Gothic baronial fantasy — it is **Hampstead Tower** of 1880–81, designed by J.T. WIMPERIS for Mr. H.F. Baxter.

Turning up the hill, a big rambling house with twin curvy Dutch gables can be seen over a wall on the left side of the road. This is **No. 61 Fitzjohn's Avenue**, with its entrance around the corner in Netherhall Gardens, by NORMAN SHAW, then at the height of his fame. It was built in 1876–78 for the celebrated painter Edwin Long RA, whose studio still juts from the house into the garden. The strong forms are typical of Shaw, but the rather loose overall composition makes it a minor work and it has been much messed up by later alterations. In 1887, Shaw built another house for Edwin Long just down the slope below the first, at No. 42 Netherhall Gardens, this time one of his most powerful designs — but that was demolished in 1937. Two of Shaw's best

28. The site of Fitzjohn's Avenue looking towards Belsize Avenue. An undated view.

houses do survive in Hampstead, however, and they will be visited shortly.

From the 1870s to the 1890s, the parts of Hampstead we have walked through — and right up into the old village — amounted to one huge building site as house after house, terrace after terrace, appeared across the fields. In winter there was mud everywhere. In the heat of summer, dust choked the inhabitants. The new houses of that time continue up the hill of Fitzjohn's Avenue. No. 69 of 1877 shows some originality, but most of the designs along this stretch are uninspired.

No. 73 is a stunningly dull house of the 1880s above the bend of the avenue, but it is notable for the boldly simplified front doorway and ground floor window added by the Arts and Crafts architect C.F.A. VOYSEY in 1901–03 for the owner P.A. Barendt. This is the only Voysey design we shall see on this walk, and it cannot adequately represent one of the most influential figures in the simplifying phase of British architecture at the turn of the century. But Voysey (1857–1941) built a fair amount in the outlying parts of Hampstead, for he lived nearby in St John's Wood during the active part of his career between 1890 and 1901. The long projecting entrance porch that he added in 1890 to Russell House, No. 71 South End Road (opposite the south end of the Heath) was one of his first works, but already his fresh white personal style is recognisable. Apart from a number of other such additions, he built the charming stone wing towards the road at No. 16 Chalcot Gardens in England's Lane (1898, then the house of the famous book illustrator Arthur Rackham) and, for his own father, Voysey did his loveliest London house, Annesley Lodge at No. 8 Platt's Lane (1896). Annesley Lodge will be visited on the second walk in this book, as will several excellent Arts and Crafts houses by other architects.

29. On the left is Fitzjohn's Primary School, built 1855–57 as the school and headmaster's house of the Soldiers' Daughters Home. On the right is the Soldiers' Daughters Home itself facing the High Street. Fitzjohn's Primary School is now behind no. 88 Fitzjohn's Avenue. (From The Times, *19th June 1857)*

Opposite 73, is no. 88 and behind that the good stone Gothic building of the Fitzjohn's Primary School, built 1855–57 as the school and headmaster's house of the Soldiers' Daughters Home, opened by the Prince Consort in June 1857. (Higher up Fitzjohn's Avenue, and just off our walk, is no. 116 which was the Sailors' Daughters Home of 1869 by an architect named Ellis, in a friendly brick Tudor manner.)

ARKWRIGHT ROAD

Returning to our walk, and continuing up Fitzjohn's Avenue to the junction with Arkwright Road, the house on the left is **Uplands**, No. 75, and was built in the 1870s for another celebrated Victorian painter, Paul Falconer Pool RA. This is the first of a group of houses by the architect THEODORE GREEN. Green's houses are big brick Gothic designs, full of odd spiky detailing and barge-boarded gables. We can see others by him around the corner in Arkwright Road, Nos. 1, 2 and 4 (for the artist F.W. Topham) all of the 1870s. There is an oddity on the top corner of Arkwright Road — housing in a sort of Neo-Victorian manner (presumably to fit in with the neighbours) built in 1977–79 for the London Borough of Camden by the architects POLLARD, THOMAS AND EDWARDS — restless but imaginative. **No. 9** (of 1874) was in Edwardian times the stately house of Sir Joseph Beecham Bart., the tycoon inventor of Beecham's pills and powders, and father of the conductor Sir Thomas. At the present time it is owned by the trade union ASLEF.

ELLERDALE ROAD

Walking down Arkwright Road and taking the first turning to the right, there are more houses by THEODORE GREEN in Ellerdale Road. Among some dull houses and a charming Queen Anne style design of 1880 at No. 7 (note the sunflower panels), No. 26 is a good example of Green's 1870s manner, while he built No. 2 for himself in *c*1890. But beside that is one of the most splendid of all Victorian town houses.

This is **No. 6 Ellerdale Road**, and it was built in 1874–76 (extended 1885) by the great NORMAN SHAW to be his own family home. Shaw (1831–1912) was born in Edinburgh and trained there by William Burn, architect of mansions for the Scottish aristocracy; he moved to London to work for Anthony Salvin and then G.E. Street (architect of the Law Courts). His own practice from 1862 onwards flourished and he became — for an architect — famous in the 1870s through a series of houses, featuring his variations on the new Queen Anne style, along Chelsea Embankment and elsewhere. From 1876 he lived in this house in Hampstead until his death, and it was in his study here that his largest works (New Scotland Yard, the White Star building in Liverpool, Bryanston in Dorset, the Gaiety Theatre, the Alliance Assurance buildings in St James's Street, the extension to Bradford Town Hall, and the magnificent frontage of the Piccadilly Hotel) were initially designed.

Shaw's own house was itself revolutionary, for it moved the Queen Anne style into a greater freedom of design. In the inventive frontage Shaw used white plastering to give visual importance to the less weighty of the two high oriels, thus balancing the two very different halves of the elevation in a subtle way. Alas, you cannot see the interiors today, unless you become a nun. But the main room on the left, with its tall windows in the projecting bay was the dining room that was the centre of general activities of the Shaw family's life. The round porthole which you can see on the exterior, on the left of that room, lit a stairway up to Shaw's own isolated 'den', where he worked and could look down into the dining room. Around the side of the house to the left can be seen the 1885 extension overlooking the garden.

In the 1950s, before the house became a nunnery, John Brandon-Jones was shown over it by the then owner, who let out rooms. In a small upper bedroom, he was introduced to Norman Shaw's son, by then aged and poor, who had returned to rent a place in his childhood home.

ARKWRIGHT ROAD continued

Retracing our steps along Ellerdale Road, we turn right down Arkwright Road again, passing No. 13 (Welford House) of the 1870s by THEODORE GREEN. Nos. 15–21 are pretty Queen Anne style artistic houses of the 1880s, much mauled by later alterations. On the corner of Frognal, No. 28 is a big lumbering Queen Anne style house of

30. R. Norman Shaw, architect, (1831–1912).

31. No. 9 Arkwright
Road, built in 1874 and
the home, in Edwardian
times, of Sir Joseph
Beecham the millionaire
pharmaceutical
manufacturer, and his
son Sir Thomas, the
famous conductor. The
house is now owned by
the trade union ASLEF.

32. No. 6 Ellerdale Road,
built 1874–76 by the
architect Norman Shaw
as his own family home
until his death in 1912.

the 1880s by R.A. BRIGGS (1858–1916), widely known as Bungalow Briggs from his book *Bungalows and Country Residences*. (At the bottom end of Arkwright Road, and over-looking the thunderous traffic of Finchley Road, is the charming Arts and Crafts Tudor building that is now the **Camden Arts Centre**, built as Hampstead Central Library in 1897, architect ARNOLD TAYLOR).

FROGNAL

Turning right here into Frognal, there is a row of quietly pleasing Queen Anne style houses on the left, Nos. 33 and 35 of 1893, No. 37 of 1888 (the great horn player Denis Brain lived here for the five years up to his tragically early death in 1956). Then comes Hampstead's third surviving house by NORMAN SHAW, **No. 39** of 1884–85, built for the much-loved illustrator of children's books, Kate Greenaway. It is a remarkable design. As we approach from this direction, the tall side elevation is seen, with soaring chimneys. Then we come opposite the frontage, not particularly strong from this viewpoint, though very pretty with all its tile-hanging. But move a few yards further, and the corner of the house opens up to reveal Kate Greenaway's high studio window in a composition of much power.

33. Kate Greenaway's house at no. 39 Frognal, built by Norman Shaw 1884–85. From here she conducted a romantic correspondence with Ruskin.

On the opposite side of the road, the architecture moves from the Queen Anne of the 1880s to the Edwardian Baroque of London's most consciously Imperial days. This is **University College School** of 1906–07 by ARNOLD MITCHELL, in a later variation of the same manner that we saw in Lloyds Bank, Rosslyn Hill. The school buildings consist of rather dumpy brickwork blocks, but they are brought to life by the flamboyantly Baroque carving of the stonework and cupolas. Inside is one of the best Edwardian Baroque halls, wooden panelled and with a curving barrel-vaulted plaster ceiling. This and much of the main block was burned down in 1978, but has been finely restored by the architect MICHAEL FOSTER. A glorious photograph exists of King Edward VII on the main entrance steps at the opening of the school. Today, the same King's robed statue stands regally in the niche above the curvaceous Baroque doorway.

34. Entrance frontage of University College School, Frognal. Designed 1906–07 by Arnold Mitchell in a full-blown Edwardian Baroque style, with a statue of Edward VII above the flamboyant main doorway.

35. The main hall of University College School, faithfully restored since the disastrous fire of 1978.

Further up Frognal are a pair of early Neo-Georgian houses of 1892 by SIR REGINALD BLOMFIELD, architect of the buildings around much of Piccadilly Circus. Blomfield himself lived in No. 51 ('a cottage', he described it), while the eminent Arts and Crafts bookbinder and printer T.J. Cobden-Sanderson, lived in No. 49. Behind Blomfield's house, but reached along a tiny alley off Frognal Lane around the corner, is an even more distinguished house by an architect for himself.

FROGNAL LANE

This is No. 42 Frognal Lane, built in 1881 as Hall Oak by BASIL CHAMPNEYS. Champneys (1842–1935) designed several excellent buildings at Oxford, the glorious Rylands Memorial Library in Manchester, Bedford College (the 1910 range) in Regent's Park (now Regent's College) and several buildings in Hampstead which we shall see on the second of these walks. He is an architect who should be better known, and his own house here off Frognal Lane is a remarkably strong composition — rising to four gables and a crowning central group of four chimneys. The house is now divided into flats.

FROGNAL WAY

Going back into Frognal, we cross the road near the site of the vanished old Hampstead Manor Farm and walk along the unpaved Frognal Way (where we should perhaps divert our purist Victorian-Edwardian eyes from good examples of varied 1930s architecture — No. 66 Frognal of 1936–38 by CONNELL, WARD AND LUCAS; No. 5 Frognal Way of 1930 by ADRIAN SCOTT brother of Sir Giles Gilbert Scott, for his own use; No. 7 of c1930 by OSWALD MILNE; No. 9, the Sun House of 1935–36 by MAXWELL FRY; No. 14 by C.H.B. QUENNELL, our first view of the work of an architect we shall hear much of in the second of these walks; No. 20, 'Blue Tiles', of 1932 by R.J. PAGE of Tomkins, Horner and Ley, for Gracie Fields). At this last green-tiled Spanishy house, Frognal Way turns left uphill and at the top we emerge into Church Row, outside the gates of Hampstead Parish Church.

HAMPSTEAD PARISH CHURCH

The **Parish Church of St John** is widely thought of as a Georgian church for the date
1745 is inscribed on its entrance front. But many of the most attractive features of its
interior were done during Victorian times, and it is good to appreciate these at the end
of this Victorian walk. The church as built by the architect JOHN SANDERSON in 1745–47
consisted of the present nave and tower. In 1843 the transepts were added and the
church was extended 30 feet westward. The altar is now at the west end — originally it
was at the traditional east, where the tower and present central entrance are.

*36. Frognal Lane,
postcard c1906.*

In 1878 the increasing population of Hampstead, in times when most people
attended church or chapel assiduously, meant that yet more space was needed for the
congregation. In that year, only an outraged petition by parishioners prevented
further changes involving the demolition of the tower. Instead, the architect F.P.
COCKERELL reoriented the church to an altar at the west end and built the present
chancel.

The decoration of the chancel was carried out in 1883 by T.G. JACKSON (1835–1924),
later Sir Graham Jackson, the eminent architect of the Oxford University Examination
Schools and many other university buildings — he was the son of a notable Hampstead family. It was Jackson who designed the pavement, organ, choir stalls, panell-
ing, chandelier and the railings (the pulpit is Georgian, cut down to its present size by
Cockerell in 1878). And it seems to have been Jackson who designed the intertwining
double gold decorative pattern that weaves over the surfaces of so much of the church,
blending the new work of his time with the old, and giving the interior of the building
much of its individual character.

At about this time, in the 1880s and 90s, many of the stained-glass windows were
added to the church. Three large ones above the altar were designed by PROFESSOR
ELLIS WOOLDRIDGE of Oxford University, and were executed by Powell. Those windows are conventional good work, done with dignity rather than fire. Much of the rest
of the stained glass was designed, executed and given to the church by ALFRED BELL,
whose fantastic Gothic house at Nos. 1 and 3 Lyndhurst Terrace was seen earlier on

37. St. John's, Hampstead Parish Church, Church Row. The Victorian chancel and galleries were added to the Georgian church in c1880 by F.P. Cockerell and given its present attractive wall and roof decoration, floor and choir stalls etc in 1883 by (Sir) T. Graham Jackson. The north chapel on the right is by Temple Moore (1912).

this walk. Bell was a partner in the leading stained glass firm of Clayton and Bell, and a zealous member of the church's congregation. He designed the painted decoration of the nave ceiling (removed in the 1950s) and the font. He also did almost all the nave and gallery windows over a number of years. Some of these are excellent work, but his best designs and subtlest colours are in the large lunette windows in the two transepts.

The final major stage of the church's building came in 1912, when one of the last great Gothic church architects, TEMPLE MOORE (1856–1920), built the vestries and other rooms around the chancel, and then the present north chapel with its imaginative rooflight. What these Victorians and Edwardians added to the old church gives it much of the character and splendour that it has today.

THE TOMB OF NORMAN SHAW

People who have followed this walk around some of the celebrated and the little-known buildings of Victorian and Edwardian Hampstead may like to pay tribute to one of its major figures. Outside the main door of the parish church, a sign points along a path to the grave of the painter John Constable, who died before Queen Victoria came to the throne. Along the same path through the churchyard is the grave of NORMAN SHAW, the leading late Victorian architect. It lies among the trees to the left of the path about halfway down the slope towards the wall. Shaw died in 1912 and his tomb-chest (in which many of his family were buried too) was designed by his pupil Ernest Newton with Laurence Turner. There is an unexpected and moving experience

38. Norman Shaw's tomb in Hampstead churchyard. His own house may be seen in the distance.

here, too. Standing beside the tomb-chest and turning to the south east, one sees a hundred yards or so away, through the trees, the fine tall garden frontage of the house Shaw built for himself (facing onto Ellerdale Road) and lived in so happily for thirty-six years. If Shaw and his fellow Victorian architects returned to Hampstead today, they would find many disorienting changes. Yet they would be pleased that the grandeur, and even the absurdities, of their designs still provide so much of the flavour of the old village.

CHURCH ROW

That homage done, we may complete this first walk around late 19th-century Hampstead by strolling along Church Row past the Georgian houses where so many of those Victorian architects lived – GEORGE GILBERT SCOTT THE YOUNGER at No. 26, GEORGE FREDERICK BODLEY at No. 24, THOMAS GARNER at No. 20 and TEMPLE MOORE at No. 16. Some famous literary figures lived here at the same period – Christopher Wade has compiled a list including H.G. Wells for three years up to 1912 at No. 17, Wilkie Collins at No. 25, Oscar Wilde's friend Lord Alfred Douglas at No. 26 (from 1907) and Compton Mackenzie at No. 28 around 1910. On the left, Gardnor Mansions (1898–99 by GEORGE SHERRIN) interrupts the Georgian row. At the end of Church Row lies the Heath Street extension cut through the narrow alleys to join Fitzjohn's Avenue in 1887–89, and we are back among the costly little boutiques that are threatening to overwhelm the heart of Hampstead today. To the right here is the way to Fitzjohn's Avenue and on down to central London. To the left, Heath Street runs fifty yards between the high Victorian buildings that replaced the old slums in about 1890, past the Liberal Club (1889 by SPALDING AND CROSS) on the right, Hampstead Mansions and the Express Dairy building (1889 by KEITH YOUNG) on the left, back to the Edwardian Hampstead Underground Station. And so home to tea and crumpets.

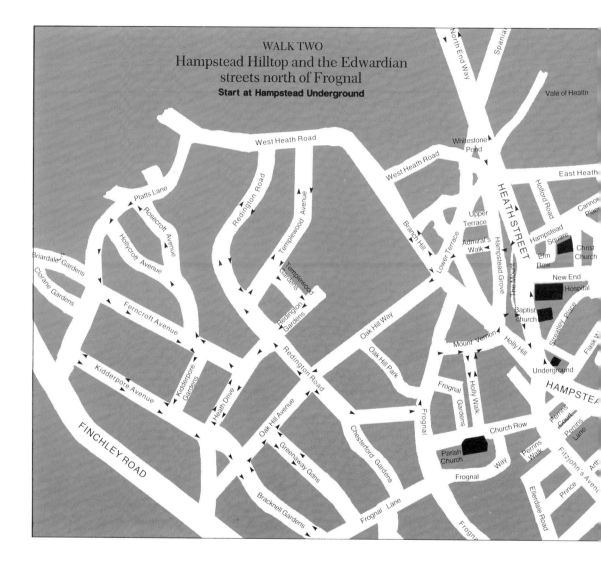

WALK TWO
Hampstead Hilltop and the Edwardian
streets north of Frognal
Start at Hampstead Underground

WALK TWO

Hampstead Hilltop and the Edwardian streets north of Frognal

The first of these two walks in Hampstead made a wide sweep east and south of the village, looking at Victorian buildings that were mostly of the early 1890s or the decades before. In the second walk, we will be following a route through the old streets of the village up towards the top of Hampstead hill, then out into the network of roads developed north and west of the High Street and Frognal. This area was still farm land until the end of the century. The streets built then are wide and well treed, as if to express the prosperity of the high years of the British Empire. The street lines snake and curl across the slopes in the new fashion of the time. Most of the roads and the buildings we shall see there — big houses of Arts and Crafts originality or Neo-Georgian vigour, churches and chapels, and a college of London University — are of the late 1890s or the Edwardian decade. The walk starts and ends at Hampstead Underground Station.

HEATH STREET — upper part

By the time King Edward VII died in 1910, the shopping streets of Hampstead village were lined by buildings of a broad variety of periods and architectural styles. Walking up Heath Street from Hampstead Station, the first three frontages on the far side of the street illustrate this. The first is the old Fire Station of 1873 in a Venetian Gothic manner, which we examined in the first walk. Then comes a small late-Georgian house, so plain that the eye scarcely takes it in. Thirdly a little building of about 1900 — hardly larger than its next-door neighbour, but action-packed with its oriel window and athletic arch rising to a Venetian window and a clever curly gable above.

The rich contrasts of style continue higher up Heath Street. Nos. 69–73 are of grey-white brick with ornate window surrounds and cornices of pre-cast artificial stone — typical mid-Victorian of the 1850s. Opposite these houses, No. 66 was built in 1900 (fifty yards down the footpath and steps beside 66, lies the charming early Victorian enclave of cottages called Mansfield Place). The splendid Horse and Groom public house, of the late 1890s, was described in the first of these two walks. A little farther up the hill, on the opposite side of Heath Street, another pub, the Nag's Head, takes us back to public house architecture of the 1850s.

Continuing up Heath Street, the narrow sliver of green land called The Mount rises beside the road on the left. Ford Madox Brown used this as the background to one of his best known pictures, *Work*, started in 1852 when he had lodgings in Heath Street. Most of the houses around The Mount are Georgian but, near the centre of the row above the green strip, **Heath Mansions** rises in four storeys of typical, if rather nondescript, Edwardian flats with many bay windows surrounded by rich red brick.

Opposite Heath Mansions, down the green slope and across the road, is **Heath Street Baptist Church** of 1860–61, architect C.J. SEARLE. The Gothic architecture of the stone frontage has a slightly wild character. It has slender traceried side windows. Between these, the central bay contains the main door, two firm buttresses and a big west window. The side bays have doors too, and buttresses rising to stepped bell-turrets and spectacular thin spires above. Beyond the Baptist Church are some very handsome Georgian and early Victorian houses. A row of shop fronts follows, and then the gateway into the rear courtyard of **New End Hospital**.

As I write this, the old hospital buildings are the subject of much controversy as to their future. The hospital was built on the site, and indeed used the old building, of the second Hampstead Workhouse which was here from 1800 and was rebuilt in 1849. The newer hospital buildings are of various dates, but by far the most striking part is on the far side of the courtyard. There is the rotunda building, with its thick piers and buttresses of brick rising past several circular storeys of ward windows to curious gables. Beside the rotunda, a massive metal water-tank towers overhead. These are designs by an architect called CHARLES BELL. They show that barbarian vigour typical of the mid-Victorian years, but in fact they were added as late as 1883–84 to the earlier ranges of 1849–50 (architect H.E. KENDALL), 1869 and 1878.

39. Heath Street Baptist Church, by C.J. Searle, 1860–61.

40. New End Hospital rotunda and water tower (1883–84), seen here from the enclave of small Victorian cottages called Mansfield Place. The architect was Charles Bell.

Those earlier parts, the main hospital entrance frontage in impure Classical style, can be seen if we leave the rear courtyard and turn right into the street called New End. On the actual corner of New End and Heath Street is the final major section added to the hospital, a range of 1905 in an Edwardian Baroque style slightly too grand for its small site. The architects here were KEITH YOUNG and HENRY HALL, a partnership that built many Edwardian hospitals — including the Royal Dental in Leicester Square, and the now-demolished Hampstead General of 1903 in Pond Street, as well as the partly surviving lower part of the Express Dairy building (1889) in Heath Street.

Continuing up Heath Street beyond The Mount and New End, there are undistinguished late-Victorian and Edwardian houses with shops to right and left, then the self-confident public house of 1854, the Coach and Horses. Opposite this there are nice Georgian houses and No. 116, an Edwardian paraphrase of a Georgian house done with a light touch in about 1910. Another Georgian house follows, and beyond that on the right, a charming Arts and Crafts gateway gives entry to a little garden in front of the Friends' Meeting House.

VICTORIAN CHURCHES IN HAMPSTEAD VILLAGE

By 1900, the main artery of Hampstead (Rosslyn Hill, High Street, Heath Street) had along its length churches or chapels of most of the major branches of Christianity. In the year of the battle of Waterloo, there had been only the two Church of England Georgian buildings in Church Row and Downshire Hill and the Rosslyn Hill Chapel (now rebuilt) for nonconformists. 1816 saw the Roman Catholic church built in Holly Place. Then came the Baptist Chapel in 1860, the new building for Unitarians in Rosslyn Hill in 1862, the Congregationalists and a new Church of England parish centre at the crossing of Pond Street and Rosslyn Hill. The Presbyterians came first to the High Street (at the corner of Willoughby Road, now demolished), and then in 1904 to the bottom of Frognal Lane, while in 1890 the Christian Science Reading Room was opened.

To these shrines of the British Christian sub-divisions, the Society of Friends or Quakers added their serene **Meeting House** in 1907 on the corner of Heath Street and an access road of Hampstead Square. The architect was FRED ROWNTREE (1860–1927), a member of the famous Quaker chocolate manufacturing family from Yorkshire. He learned his profession in Scarborough and Glasgow, then took up the Arts and Crafts Free Style shortly after 1890 when Voysey and others started to attract so much attention to that simple and graceful approach. For the next twenty years, Rowntree designed a series of Friends' Meeting Houses and domestic work around the country, as well as an insurance office in Cheapside and a newspaper building in Fleet Street, both now vanished. After the 1914–18 war, Rowntree involved himself in a typically Quaker enterprise making prefabricated buildings in Belgium to replace the countless houses destroyed in that country by the warring German and British armies.

That idealism of spirit shows in Rowntree's design for Hampstead. The approach through a garden is an inspiration in itself, making a green transition from the traffic noise of Heath Street. The front of the Meeting House reinforces this change of atmosphere by welcoming the visitor into the white-walled house via a strong timber porch with a rounded roof, a half dome of grey-green copper suspended above it. Inside the building, after a small lobby, is a grave white hall, not large, but of quiet beauty, with touches of Arts and Crafts detailing and a motif of shallow arches around the walls. Leaving the Meeting House, it is worthwhile to look at the outside of the building along its flank. The influence of Voysey is very much there in the white walls, tall chimneys, band windows and pretty gables. But there are Classical touches that, in their setting, make one smile. Rowntree makes the Arts and Crafts style convincingly his own.

41. Friends' Meeting House, Heath Street. Designed in 1907 by Fred Rowntree, himself a Quaker, in a variation of the white-walled Arts and Crafts manner initiated by C.F.A. Voysey.

42. The Oil Painting Room at Inverforth House, formerly The Hill, North End Way. (From The Architects Journal, 18 Nov 1925).

THE HILL (INVERFORTH HOUSE)

Before continuing the route of the main walk, I want to offer readers an optional extra — an offshoot up Heath Street, past Queen Mary's Nursing Home (1921 on the right), past the Whitestone Pond (on the left) and down North End Way (towards Golders Green) to see **Inverforth House**, also known as The Hill.

This large mansion stands in its own wide gardens, back behind a wall on the left side of North End Way. The present grandiose building is nothing like the original house built on the site in 1807 by the banking magnate Samuel Hoare (who lived in Heath House, opposite the pub Jack Straw's Castle, just up the road). The house was named The Hill and it stayed in the Hoare family till about 1894, providing their headquarters for the fight to save Hampstead Heath from developers. Then it was sold and rebuilt, and sold again in 1906 to the Lancashire grocer turned soap millionaire, William Hesketh Lever, who became in 1917 Lord Leverhulme, chairman of the huge corporation Lever Brothers (later called Unilever).

The giant house as it stands today is on a scale doubtless felt proper for the London residence of one of the wealthiest of Edwardian tycoons. What can be seen is mostly the work of three architects. All were men who also designed much of Lord Leverhulme's model northern industrial town beside the Mersey, Port Sunlight. Firstly, G.H. GRAYSON (1871–1951) of the partnership Grayson and Ould rebuilt the central block in 1906–10, using the vernacular manner in soft red brick and hung tiles made fashionable by Norman Shaw. It is nothing much from the entrance side, but the garden elevation has a two-storey frontage with a fine tall roof and dormer windows. A huge chimney and a glazed observatory tower dominate the skyline.

Next, SEGAR OWEN (b.1874) altered and enlarged the house in 1914, giving it much of the appearance we see today, and J. LOMAX-SIMPSON did further work. Between them, these two architects did the stone columned covered terrace in front of the main block on the garden side and the one-storey wings (now spoiled by hospital structures on top) that project towards the garden. Unlike the stylistic simplicity of the central block, these additions are all in some kind of Classical style, with many Ionic columns of stone of red rubbed brickwork.

The Edwardian garden of The Hill was laid out in 1906–10 by THOMAS MAWSON, one of the foremost garden designers-cum-architects of the time. Mawson's designs included the famous pergola walk, now open to the public, on the Hampstead Heath side of the grounds. From the pergola's magical raised walkway, there is a view of the main garden frontage of The Hill.

Later, Lord Leverhulme acquired more land north of The Hill, built a bridge over a public lane that he failed to persuade the London County Council to close, and employed LESLIE MANSFIELD in the 1920s to design further gardens (now open to the public under the name of The Hill via an entrance farther down North End Way). (*Information from Edward Hubbard, architectural historian of Leverhulme's empire*).

After Leverhulme's death in 1925, the house was bought by Lord Inverforth and when he died The Hill was presented to Manor House Hospital in 1956. The Hospital (which is run by Trades Unions) changed the name of the house to Inverforth House and used it initially as a women's branch. At present, it is used as a convalescent home and many of the wards are closed for lack of demand. Fortunately, the interiors are in good order. The entrance hall is richly decorated with painting and relief sculpture. On the right of the entrance, a fairly small but magnificently carved marble staircase rises to a first floor landing surrounded by fine carved doorways. Back on the ground floor the hall gives onto an elegantly painted saloon and a darkly panelled dining room. Both of these open onto the covered terrace and the garden beyond. To the left of the hall, marbled passages, stairways and vestibules lead down to the underground ballroom.

43. George du Maurier, writer and artist (1834–96), who lived in no. 28 Hampstead Grove.

44. Sir George Gilbert Scott, foremost architect of the Gothic revival, (1811–78), who lived in Admiral's House.

THE MOUNT SQUARE

Returning to the main walk in Heath Street, our route crosses the street opposite the Friends' Meeting House where a small lane leads a few yards through to **The Mount Square**. Nos. 1–3 of this tiny square form a pretty Victorian row, while the rest of the small houses around it (except No. 16, which is of this century) are Georgian workmen's brick cottages that were slums until modern times.

Above The Mount Square loom the rear walls of Old Grove House and New Grove House, both of which face onto Hampstead Grove (Nos. 26 and 28) on the other side. Moving around to the entrances of these two houses, it is apparent that Old Grove House is another of the early Georgian gentlemen's houses of Hampstead, while No. 28 is in a Tudor style dating from about 1840 — though the Victorian work only covered over an existing house said to have been a windmill. It was in this Tudorised building, New Grove House, that the novelist (*Trilby* and other books) and *Punch* cartoonist George du Maurier lived until 1895. It was divided into flats in 1986.

ADMIRAL'S WALK

Crossing over Hampstead Grove, we go along the short length of Admiral's Walk and pause outside **Admiral's House**, which rears up in Georgian but eccentric forms on the right. Our pause is not to imagine a retired naval officer pacing the roof throughout the Napoleonic Wars with telescope under arm as if it were his ship's quarterdeck, but to salute the shade of a later owner. SIR GEORGE GILBERT SCOTT, designer of the Albert Memorial, St Pancras Station's frontage and hotel, the Foreign Office in Whitehall — and pitiless restorer of many ruined medieval churches, to the fury of William Morris and his circle — lived here in the 1850s and 60s, at the height of his career. The famous man who 'corrected' so many Gothic churches by stripping out historical encrustations, did not meddle with the Georgian oddities of the Admiral's House. So no reprimand is called for if we glimpse Scott's craggy features at a window of this odd building.

Next door, at an angle to Admiral's House, is another whose age would be hard to guess from what can be seen. This is **Grove Lodge**, whose most famous owner, John Galsworthy, moved here in 1918 and wrote the later volumes of the *Forsyte Saga* in the house. Next we pass on the left the mouth of a path so green that it might be in deepest rural Herefordshire (it leads to an interesting studio cottage called *Rickford Lodge*, built in 1931 by SIR EDWARD MAUFE, architect of Guildford Cathedral).

LOWER TERRACE

This part of Hampstead is the village at its most leafy and picturesque, with Georgian cottages and mansions set at all angles in the hilly lanes. Up to the right lies the fresh water reservoir built as a commercial venture in 1856. There are also the remains of some handsome Victorian houses of the 1880s in Lower Terrace, Upper Terrace and Judge's Walk. backing onto the fine northward view from the edge of Hampstead Heath here. These remnants include **Hawthorne House** in Lower Terrace, built in 1883 as Tudor House by ERNEST GEORGE AND PETO for W.J. Goode, the owner of Goode's, the famous china shop in Mayfair, and butchered during its transformation into a Christian Science nursing home in 1959. This house, at the time of writing, is about to be demolished. **Upper Terrace Lodge**, designed by BASIL CHAMPNEYS in 1882 for its site at the west end of Upper Terrace, was altered by him in 1888 and extended at the rear by LUTYENS in the 1920s. Upper Terrace house is an old house refronted by OLIVER HILL in the 1920s and further altered by FORBES AND TATE.

We turn left for the short distance down Lower Terrace, noticing **No. 12** on the left, which has charming Edwardian Arts and Crafts additions and relief sculpture added to a basically Georgian house. The designer of the Edwardian additions is unknown, though the last owner of the large nearby house The Grange (now demolished), a Mr. Inman, said that the *Art Nouveau* work in both houses was done by an uncle of his. Off our route, just along the lane called Windmill Hill, are Nos. 1–6, a row of semi-detached houses of 1894, the work of the builder Charles B. King.

BRANCH HILL and the CONSUMPTION HOSPITAL

At the bottom of Lower Terrace, we meet Branch Hill at right angles. Standing on this corner, to the left — across a little valley — is the great Victorian bulk of the old **Consumption Hospital**, now the National Institute for Biological Standards and Control. We may want to walk forty yards to the left to get a better view of the buildings. This ponderous dreadnought, done in the manner of a retarded Loire *chateau*, was the result of an architectural competition held in 1877 for the North London Hospital for Consumption to be sited here in Hampstead's healthy high air. Consumption, or tuberculosis, was still of course one of the great killer illnesses of Victorian Britain. Several distinguished architects, whose works we can enjoy elsewhere in Hampstead, entered the competition — Batterbury and Huxley, Henry Legg, John McKean Brydon. Some of their designs would probably have been more pleasing than that of the winner, T. ROGER SMITH, who is not really a name or a talent to light up the spirit (though Andrew Saint tells me he was thought good at sanitation and was influential in Bombay). Smith's design of a single great brick block — with its stone dressings, pepperpot turrets, tall pinnacles and chimneys giving a little relief — was built in three vertical chunks opened respectively in 1880, 1892 and 1903. No more was then done until 1929, after it had been converted into the National Institute for Medical Research. At that time the extension to the northern end was added to designs by MAXWELL AYRTON, whose work for the great civil engineer Owen Williams we shall see at No. 16 Redington Road (Ayrton was the partner of Sir John Simpson — together with Owen Williams, they designed the Empire Pool, Wembley). Here, at the hospital in Hampstead, Ayrton did one of his most distinguished works. His dramatic bridge, on several storeys, separates his block from Smith's Victorian work. The

45. *The garden frontage of the former Consumption Hospital, Windmill Hill, designed 1877–1903 by T. Roger Smith with, on the left a 1929 extension by Maxwell Ayrton. The building has more recently been the National Institute for Biological Standards and Control.*

46. *Branch Hill Lodge in 1899.*

extension itself has a severe elegance to its tall brickwork forms.

We now turn back the short distance to the corner of Lower Terrace and cross the road called Branch Hill. This is one of the oldest routes in Hampstead, an almost straight continuation of the steep way up High Street and Holly Hill, running over the ridge top and (at the stretch we meet here) on to West Heath Road, which snakes along the edge of Hampstead Heath. That is not the route we shall follow, but as we cross the road notice the vigorous Gothic of the entrance lodge to Branch Hill Lodge, the big house inside the grounds. The entrance lodge (the date on it is 1868) is often attributed to s.s. TEULON, the architect of St Stephen's Church, Haverstock Hill, and the style fits quite well even if the documentary evidence is missing. Beyond the gates, the drive curls through the grounds to the monstrous house, **Branch Hill Lodge** itself.

There has been a series of houses on this spot since the first in the early 1700s. The second was designed by HENRY FLITCROFT in 1745 for a pre-eminent judge. It was later lived in by a Lord Chancellor (the Earl of Rosslyn, who gave his name to Rosslyn Hill) and, later still, by Byron's estranged wife. It is said that Teulon rebuilt the house in the 1870s, but if so his design too was replaced by the present lumpish exterior in 1901 (the date appears several times high on the gables). The architect of this disgrace to Edwardian architecture is not established, but it was probably commissioned by Robert Nivison JP, who was the first owner listed after that date. Now, it is an old people's home and most of the large garden down the slope beyond it is filled by an interesting low-rise concrete housing estate designed in the 1960s by GORDON BENSON and ALAN FORSYTH of Camden Borough Architects' Department, which attracted much attention when it was built in 1974–76.

OAK HILL WAY

Doing our best to forget Branch Hill's lapse in standards of Victorian and Edwardian design, we walk a few yards down the slope outside the entrance gates of Branch Hill Lodge and enter a surprisingly formal gateway into a country lane. This is Oak Hill Way, which runs several hundred yards through woodland that was until 1960 part of the Oak Hill Park estate. The last owner of the estate was a famous publisher, Sir Stanley Unwin of George Allen and Unwin, whose small figure could still be seen bounding around the tennis court beside this lane well into the 1950s.

Oak Hill Way is fenced, but unpaved and rough, and a pedestrian-only barrier at its half-way point means that the only cars to use it are those of the few who live here. As we walk its length, picking our way past the pot-holes or puddles, we pass on the right an isolated house called **Combe Edge** (dated 1874 and almost totally hidden behind its wall), where a plaque carries the name of a successful, though now largely forgotten, children's novelist Elizabeth Rundle Charles. Opposite it is another house (of the 1960s, designed by JAMES CUBITT) but nothing else except the barrier and the site of the old tennis court stands near the muddy path through the woods. There are two more houses and two blocks of flats, then the lane narrows to a footpath and drops suddenly forty yards down the hill to join Redington Road.

REDINGTON ROAD — entering EDWARDIAN HAMPSTEAD

The earliest part of Redington Road lies to the left here. The street was set out from 1875, when the Maryon Wilson family, lords of the manor of Hampstead, sold the land. It has some important late-Victorian houses which we will see later, but for the present our walk turns to the right.

At once, we find ourselves in truly Edwardian Hampstead. On the far side of the road, No. 39 Redington Road is a big house in a wild version of the Arts and Crafts Free Style, standing on the corner of Oak Hill Avenue. The elevations are compositions of areas of brick and others of roughcast. One gable has a large lunette window. The corner has a turret with a looping balustrade and a dome. Another gable has relief sculpture in plaster and a pretty weather vane. Every one of these features speaks of

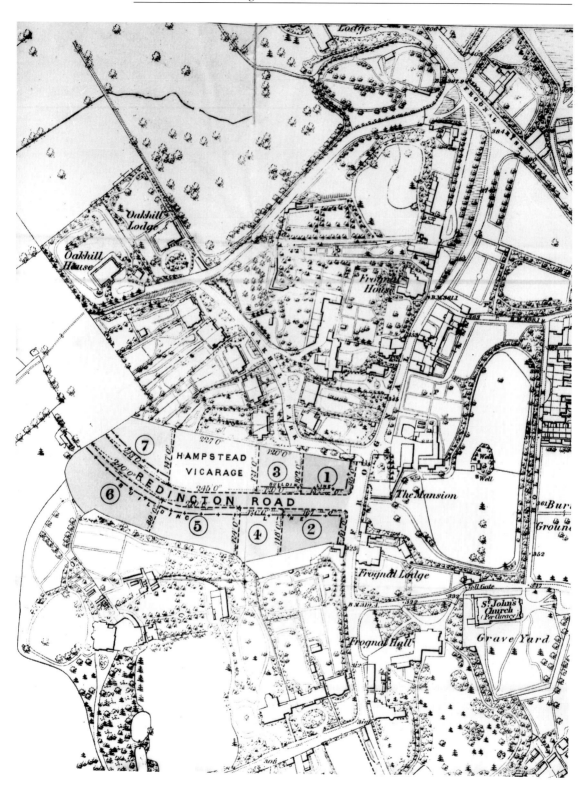

the turn of the century and a cartouche gives the date 1903. Susan Beattie has established that the house was built by Bull and Esdaile for a Miss Gibson, and the designer was probably Walter William Bull, a pupil of the *avant garde* Arts and Crafts architect, James MacLaren.

On the other side of the road, Nos. 24 and 26 are large Edwardian houses. No. 28 is a tall athletic house of *c*1907, reminiscent of the architect Arnold Mitchell. No. 30 looks oddly out of the time sequence of the street. With its big barge-board gables, it may be by Theodore Green (see his houses of the 1880s in Arkwright Road).

C.H.B. QUENNELL AND GEORGE WASHINGTON HART

The next house down the slope on the western (left-hand) side of Redington Road is the first into Quennell-land, the large area of Hampstead whose whole character is set by the many houses built to the designs of the architect c.h.b. quennell. Charles Quennell (1872–1935) was articled to a minor firm and then completed his training in the 1890s in two distinguished offices with very different approaches to architecture. First he worked under John M. Brydon, while that important originator of the Edwardian Baroque style was rebuilding and extending the Guildhall in Bath, as well as designing the Chelsea Polytechnic and Public Library. Quennell moved on to work as an assistant to Harry Wilson, one of the great original talents of Arts and Crafts architecture, who had practised with the church designer J.D. Sedding and then continued Sedding's practice after the older man's death in 1891 — in the mid-1890s, Wilson was designing and supervising the marvellous furnishings for Sedding's masterpiece Holy Trinity Church in Sloane Street, while carrying out several other commissions of his own. So, when Quennell started practice on his own account in 1896, he had experienced working in both the vigorous classicism and the free originality of the two main design streams of the period. This background shows in various ways in his many Hampstead houses.

The commission that launched Quennell's practice was a house in Hampstead for his brother William, perhaps No. 1 Rosecroft Avenue (illustrated in *The Builder* magazine in 1899). The work on site for that commission may have led to a meeting with the Irish builder-developer George Washington Hart, who was about to start a sixteen-year series of well over a hundred high-quality houses in this part of Hampstead. All of these seem to have been designed by Quennell, who was appointed by Hart as architect to this 'West Hampstead Estate' in 1898 and held the post until 1914. In that time, he produced series after series of excellent designs, most of them of two subtly varied styles, with occasional larger houses of spectacular inventiveness interspersed among them.

From 1896 until about 1920, the Hampstead Manor Estate either sold off these fields in areas large enough for half a dozen or more house plots, or else gave developers options on such pieces to be taken up over a number of years. In 1896, George Hart took up some land on both sides of part of Platt's Lane and appears to have named the new streets to lead off it. They were called Briardale and Clorane Gardens (both to the north of Platt's Lane), together with Rosecroft, Hollycroft and Ferncroft Avenues (running south and east of Platt's Lane). Hart did not build the houses on all the plots along these streets (for example, Nos. 1–31 and all even numbers of Hollycroft Avenue were built by a contractor called W.J. King of No. 7 Heath Street and not designed by Quennell). Nor did building work always proceed systematically from one end of a street to the other. But, stretch by stretch, year after year, Hart and Quennell's houses filled most of one road and then another. In tracing which are Hart-Quennell houses, I owe much to the help of Neil Burton and John Brandon-Jones.

Quennell and Hart began with a short stretch of Platt's Lane and the ends nearest to it of the roads already mentioned. Of Clorane Gardens only Nos. 12–18 appear to be

47. The estate agents' map of the proposed development area around the marked out Redington Road, in 1875. Note the many mansions and also the toll gate near St. John's Church.

Quennell's, but almost all of Briardale Gardens consists of his *c*1897 designs (using contemporary Arts and Crafts detailing) for two types of semi-detached pairs. These and the *c*1898 houses at Nos. 29–39 Platt's Lane, show promise but some design weaknesses. The magazine *The British Architect* illustrated in 1898 a selection of his Hampstead houses — that was an achievement, for it was one of the three publications followed by the many talented young architects of the time. Nos. 18 to 24 Platt's Lane and the first houses around the corner in Ferncroft Avenue date from 1899–1900 and show Quennell working out his mature manner. He blossomed from that time as Hart built along the length of Ferncroft Avenue on both sides and more houses in Platt's Lane (Nos. 41–47 of 1903).

From 1904 they then moved on to building stretches of Redington Road and Heath Drive, spreading into Oakhill Avenue and one side of Kidderpore Gardens in 1906, taking on more plots in all these roads in 1907–09, then on into Redington and Templewood Gardens, and along the length of Templewood Avenue in 1910–14.

There are good houses designed by Quennell and built by Hart elsewhere in Hampstead. But it is above all in the area bounded by Finchley Road and Platt's Lane to the west, by Frognal Lane and Branch Hill to the east, that their score upon score of fine houses, in broad streets with ample trees and gardens, set the standard of an excellent Edwardian suburban environment that has been little damaged by later developers. This Quennell-land area forms the most valuable part of the new Frognal Redington Conservation Area designated by the Borough in July 1985.

REDINGTON ROAD — central and northern sections

Returning to our walk at the point reached in Redington Road, Nos. 41–49 are a series of detached houses built in 1907–08 that serve as a good introduction to Quennell's standards of design. He had two favoured styles which he effectively set off against each other to provide contrast. One of these was descended from Norman Shaw's Queen Anne style — a restrained Arts and Crafts vernacular (sometimes called a Free Style because it is not drawn from any historical textbook style such as Classicism, Romanesque or Gothic) with walls of soft orange-red brick and upper storeys of hung tiles. The other was a domestic Edwardian kind of Classicism — in its weightier forms a simplified Baroque, otherwise a lighter Neo-Georgian. Both were used by countless Edwardian architects, but by few with more distinction than Quennell.

Key features in his designs are cleverness in planning for restricted sites, ingenious compositions of entrances and varied gables, a choice of attractive bricks in soft reds and oranges, and brilliance in the detail of brickwork in rusticated pilasters, chimneys, gables and other features. No. 41 Redington Road is an excellent start, one of the larger houses and a pleasing design with broad bays and gables advancing on both sides as well as some subtle brickwork detailing. No. 43 is another nice design, vernacular English with a big central seven-sided bay window and a clever doorway. No. 45 is quieter, with Baroque touches in the brick rusticated corners and an oriel window — Henry Brooke, controversial Home Secretary in Harold Macmillan's government, lived here with his family from the 1940s until the 70s. No. 47 is a narrower variation of No. 43, and No. 49 generally Classical again, emphasising the corner by placing a strong gable (embracing a chimney stack) and an amusingly indirect porch there.

Here Redington Road reaches the bottom of its slope and then rises again. Crossing the road at the top of Heath Drive, the corner house facing us is dated 1899, and the paucity of its design (architect, if any, unknown) and building craftsmanship bring home by contrast the sheer quality of Quennell and Hart's contemporary work. We continue up the curving hill of Redington Road and immediately find another row of Quennell-designed houses on the left. These were built in 1904–05, a little earlier than the first series in this street. No. 51 is a frothy converted Edwardian coach-house, Nos. 53 and 55 a semi-detached pair in a conventional Edwardian Neo-Georgian mode,

48. A model Edwardian bathroom c1906, by Beaver and Sons of Westminster and Gloucester.

49. Some of the new Edwardian houses took advantage of electricity in the kitchen. This design of 1912 was 'unlike the old-time kitchen with its wasteful open fireplace as anything could possibly be. Here not merely the oven, boiler and hot-plate are connected with the electric circuit, but even the kettles and frying-pans.'

50. Detail of an
Edwardian bedroom
(c1902) by George
Walton.

51. Electric cooking
apparatus became fairly
widespread after 1910 —
'new inventions have
largely reduced the
expenses, and its perfect
cleanliness recommends
it to all who can afford
the high intial cost of the
vessels.'

with typical five-light bay windows. No. 57 has been largely ruined by modern windows, but No. 59 is a pretty Neo-Georgian house with an unusual grouping of a dormer window and two chimneys at the centre of the roof. No. 61 is a quieter Neo-Georgian (Hugo Young KC lived here in 1914), and then No. 63 is a really nice Arts and Crafts design in vernacular brick and a tile-hung first floor. No. 65 is a very ambitious design in purplish brick with red trim and nice brickwork patterning — John Murray FRIBA, architect of the Crown Commissioners' Baroque offices in Whitehall, was living here in 1910. No. 67 is entirely different, much quieter and dominated by a five-light angled bay window rising through two floors. And that completes this sequence of 1904–05 Quennell houses.

Redington Road curls to the right as it rises here. On the left is another Edwardian house, No. 69, its architect unknown. Its white roughcast walls, shallow buttresses and long horizontal windows are clearly influenced by Voysey, yet Voysey himself would have done it quite differently.

There follows another run of detached houses by Quennell, Nos. 71–77. As often with his houses, it is the overall design of the group, rather than individual buildings, that does most to give warmth and distinction to the whole surroundings.

Among this handsome group of 1907–08, slightly later than the previous lot, two or three houses need special comment. No. 73 was owned by a psychiatrist called Dr. Couch, according to John Brandon-Jones. No. 75 is an ambitious design, but a little stiff — here, as occasionally in other parts of Hampstead one feels that the pressure on Quennell for new designs resulted in some that were not quite worked out. Nos. 77 and 79 are charming and relaxed compositions, the first Neo-Georgian with shutters, the second in the vernacular free style.

For some reason, the rest of this side of Redington Road was not built on until after the Great War of 1914–18. No. 81 was built in 1921 for a Mr. Haliburton-Smith to the Stripped Classical designs of SIR EDWARD MAUFE, later the architect of Guildford Cathedral and St Columba's Church, Pont Street. No. 87 was an important house in a curvacious English brick version of International Modern, done in 1938 by the clever OLIVER HILL for Juanita Francis (the well-known campaigner for women's rights) but spoiled by another architect's blockish additions of the 1970s. Beyond this, the big houses (Nos. 89–97) return to a routine version of Quennell's Neo-Georgian style, but date from 1926, long after he had ended his work in Hampstead. Their designer is not known.

However, the Hart-Quennell series did continue on the east side of Redington Road. Nos. 54–64 form part of their next series, all built in 1908–09. Again the architect mixes brick and tile-hung vernacular houses with others in a brick classical mode for variety. No. 56 has some brickwork detail in a witty travesty of classical decoration. No. 58 has been spoiled by alterations. No. 64 is a characteristic Baroque design of 1909, done with easy magnificence as if the work of a relaxed Edwardian Vanbrugh.

Beyond it lies a most extraordinary house, not by Quennell. No. 66 Redington Road (1902) is called **The Wabe**, a reference to Lewis Carroll's poem *Jabberwocky*. The house was designed for his own use by DR. WILLIAM GARNETT, Education Adviser of the London County Council in the Edwardian period. Garnett was much involved with William Lethaby and, as Secretary of the Technical Education Board, with the estab-

52. The Wabe, 66 Redington Road. Designed eccentrically for himself in 1902 by Dr William Garnett, who was Education Adviser of the London County Council. However odd the plan and design (the name is a reference to the nonsense poem Jabberwocky)*, its materials and building quality are of the high standard of Edwardian work.*

53. Magnolia Court, 70 Redington Road. Built 1912–14, probably one of Quennell's last designs. It is very grand neo-Georgian, but with the stiff formality that overtook the style just before the Great War.

lishment of the Central School of Arts and Crafts in Southampton Row. One imagines that the design of The Wabe would have made his friend Lethaby smile affectionately, for it is a functional design for an eccentric's use. The building materials are consistent with its neighbours, using brick and hung tiles. But the effect is extremely unusual — the plan is odd, big bay windows project with total disregard for visual composition, a wide terrace on top of the house gives it a flat roof surrounded by Tudor crenellation and complex chimneys. Garnett only lived in the house for about 10 years — by 1914 he had moved to The Chestnuts, nearby in Branch Hill.

After this excitement, No. 68 seems dull — it was in 1905 the only house (Heathside) at this end, apart from The Wabe, with riding stables between it and the Heath. The street reaches its last point of real interest with No. 70 (Magnolia Court). This is one of the largest survivors of Quennell's Hampstead houses and completes the time sequence of his designs along Redington Road. It was built in 1912–14 and has that almost lifeless grandiosity seen in many architects' work as the Great War approached.

As well as his work here, Quennell designed 16 houses in Hampstead Garden Suburb and half a dozen at Bickley in Kent. Leaving aside minor works, he designed one church (St John the Evangelist, Upper Edmonton, in 1907) and in 1911 a boys' prep. school called Mowden in a pleasing Arts and Crafts style on the downs overlooking Brighton (demolished *c*1960). But his major architectural monument is this part of Hampstead, whose best houses will come later on this walk. After 1914, Quennell went on to the second major achievement of his life. He (now in his forties) and his wife Marjorie moved to the country in 1920 and started to compile the much-loved series of Everyday Life books, starting with *A History of Everyday Things in England*. Their son Peter continued the literary tradition.

Retracing our route, back down Redington Road, we pass Nos. 52 and 48 on the east side. These are of 1906, perhaps designed by Quennell but both hamfistedly altered beyond recognition. No. 46 is a quirky Arty-Crafty mess, with two half-timbered gables, one of them on stubby columns. That brings us back to the corner of Templewood Avenue, where we turn left.

TEMPLEWOOD AVENUE

Templewood Avenue first appears on the Hampstead maps as late as 1909. On the right, as we come into the street, is the entrance front of the big house called No. 42 Redington Road, with a rather showy stone porch and Venetian window clipped on later to a basically decent design. From there on, it seems that Quennell designed all the original houses in the road, on left and right. Nos. 1 and 3 on the left are restrained (1910), Nos. 2 and 4 on the right (1910–11) are in a richer Neo-Georgian mood. No. 5 is a crowded Neo-Georgian design, though it has the Quennell trademarks of relief brick patterning on the chimneys and the tall narrow porch he seemed to favour at this time. Between Nos. 5 and 6 is an infill studio house of 1961 by the architect Trevor Dannatt. Then come Nos. 7, 9 and 11, again Quennell designs of 1910.

On the other side of the road Nos. 6–14 are good Quennell-Hart detached houses of 1910–11. No. 14 is an excellent example of the architect working in a free Baroque manner, a little reminiscent of Vanbrugh or Thomas Archer in the early 1700s. The house has two projecting wings and a central part that advances with a broken pediment. There are rather jokey Venetian windows in the wings on the ground floor and a number of other light-hearted Classical references.

Opposite No. 14 is a major Quennell design, one of the most striking houses in Hampstead. This is **No. 15 Templewood Avenue**, a tall elegant house standing back from the street in its own double-plot gardens. The date is unclear, but the house appears in Quennell's book of his own designs (*Modern Suburban Houses*, published by Batsford in 1906) and so it seems that it must have been built in 1905. Its composition is dominated, as seen from the road, by a tall and complex chimney stack, richly textured by projecting brickwork patterns. A short driveway through the garden leads to a

54. No. 14 Templewood Avenue (1910–11) by C.H.B. Quennell.

55. No. 15 Templewood Avenue, built c1904. It is one of Quennell's boldest house designs.

half-courtyard with the front door on the right of the house, partly enclosed by the 'Motor House' or garage, a novelty in the 1900s. From this courtyard, steps and a path lead around the terraces of the lyrical garden past the front of the house and to the far side. This garden side elevation of the house is very complicated, a composition of many varied windows and a romantic loggia balcony off the drawing room. In the design, Quennell plays visual games with the unconventional shape of the house, its projecting roofs and the changing texture of the elevations as one moves around it.

Beyond No. 15 there are no Edwardian houses left in Templewood Avenue. On the left, there are some pleasantly nondescript later houses, and then the famous **Schreiber house** (1963–64) and domed swimming pool (1968) designed by JAMES GOWAN in glass and dark-blue brick on the corner with West Heath Road. On the right, a lane called Grange Gardens has appeared beside No. 14, leading into the wildly vivacious luxury estate of houses and flats in mature woodland, built 1983–87 on the site of Quennell's biggest house. This was Temple Hill House (1913, demolished 1984). We go back down Templewood Avenue and turn left into Templewood Gardens.

56. *Oak Tree House,
Redington Gardens. It
was built in 1873 by
Basil Champneys for the
artist Henry Holiday.*

TEMPLEWOOD GARDENS AND REDINGTON GARDENS

The few houses in Templewood Gardens (*c*1912) are pleasing and the row Nos. 1–4 Redington Gardens are dignified though not inspired works of 1915–17, built by Hart and perhaps designed by Quennell (if so, shortly before his retirement as estate architect in 1914). No. 1 Templewood Gardens has the most individuality, a frail shuttered Neo-Georgian work with the front door in an inner angle and an oddly narrow central gable.

Better than that, indeed one of the star houses of north London, is the house at the far end of Redington Gardens and along a short drive. This is the magnificent **Oak Tree House**, built by one of Hampstead's resident major architects, BASIL CHAMPNEYS, in 1873 for the eminent Victorian artist Henry Holiday (1829–1937). The house is a fine lofty brickwork cube, with tall main windows and dormer windows soaring higher still. Gladstone, William Morris, the Pankhursts and other prominent Victorians visited Holiday here. It has been well converted into flats by Camden Council.

We leave Redington Gardens by the end opposite Oak Tree House (noting modern infill houses on the left), cross Redington Road and start down Heath Drive.

HEATH DRIVE

Going down the slope of Heath Drive, the houses on the right are on plots that were sold off individually or in pairs from 1890 onwards. They are of mixed design quality, many quite interesting but only one or two of real excellence. So the description of this section of the walk will only list them briefly in order from the bottom end of Heath Drive, where it rises from Finchley Road. Nos. 1–2 and 3–4 are florid semi-detached pairs of *c*1890; 5–6 a little later; 7 taking on the Neo-Georgian style. Above the corner with Kidderpore Avenue, No. 8 is a big shambling house of no quality, built for a Portuguese client, José de Sola Pinto, in *c*1900; 10a is a pretty insertion of *c*1930, in the style of Edward Maufe; 11 is a lumbering Jacobean house called Ye Gables, with three bays of wild windows, its walls now plastered over; 11a is another later insertion; 12 a quirky little house of *c*1900; 13–14 are a wretched Edwardian semi-detached pair, with nice wrought-iron porches, that were built in *c*1900 for, respectively, Isaac Gundelfinger — who changed his name to Isaac Gundle shortly before war with Germany in 1914 — and Julius Koppenhagen — the names are a reminder that there were many wealthy immigrants from persecution in central Europe at this time. No. 15 is a big messy house, called Ferncroft in Edwardian times, on the corner with Ferncroft Avenue. Above this are two more semi-detached pairs, both of 1904–05 — Nos. 16–17 in the quiet manner of the time with brick, roughcast and tile-hung areas of wall, and Nos. 18–19 an odd composition with coarse detailing. Then on the corner with Redington Road, there is No. 20 of 1905, in a naughty version of Arts and Crafts free

57. No. 33 Heath Drive, built in 1905. One of Quennell's best house designs.

style, with brick lower level and roughcast above, many stained-glass windows, nasty cornices and wavy gables — but not well built.

Our attention, as we walk down the right-hand pavement of Heath Drive, will be on the series of twelve houses, designed by Quennell and built by Hart, on the other side of the road. For these houses, Nos. 22–33 Heath Drive, all built between 1905 and 1907, are (together with three or four other individual houses) the peak of Quennell's hundred and more Edwardian designs in Hampstead. No. 22, which we see first, is an excellent free design in the architect's English vernacular style, with orange brick making a diaper pattern in the dark purplish walls. No. 23 is a bold work — it has three tile-hung gables, the outer ones projecting with 5–angled bay windows below. No. 24 is in a Neo-Georgian style — a gem of a house with especially pretty ground floor windows, though a bit spoiled by the garage extension. Nos. 25–26 are a variety of an almost standard Quennell semi-detached design, with two bold bay windows from projecting wings. (No. 25 was the home from 1910 onwards of Thomas Wise, wizard forger of rare manuscripts). No. 27 is a detached house, particularly charming with a brick central section between two white bay windows, and lines of shells embedded in its trio of white gables. Nos. 28–29 are a semi-detached pair, with a bay window of the kind that is one of Quennell's trademarks. All of the above houses date from 1907. No. 30 is another attractive and original Neo-Georgian house, with one bay window in the centre, now divided into two dwellings. Nos. 31–32 are semi-detached of 1905, very like Nos. 28–29 but notice how subtly Quennell varied the design.

The last of this row is **No. 33**, an ambitious and special corner house, among the most excellent of all his works. It dates from 1905 and is illustrated by three plates in Quennell's folio book, *Modern Surburban Houses*. The plan is clever (Neil Burton tells me that Clough Williams-Ellis said that Quennell's designs were admired by young architects of the time as examples of good planning). Still, it is the composition of the volumes of the house and its elevations (which take full advantage of the corner site) that are memorable. The brickwork of the walls and the windows are familiar Quennell components. But he placed a powerful and extraordinary four-arched open porch on the corner and then built up the whole composition to rise in both directions from

58. *Detail of no. 33 Heath Drive, showing the ingenious porch.*

it. To the left, the walls spread to one of Quennell's grand two-storey 6-angled bay windows, with a gable of patterned brickwork above. To the right of the porch, the design climbs steeply to a high double gable, reminiscent of some Lethaby houses, with more of the abstract (or, quite possibly, symbolic) brickwork relief patterns.

FERNCROFT AVENUE

Our walk returns from here some forty yards up Heath Drive and turns west up another slope into Ferncroft Avenue. With the exception of Nos. 25, 27, 43 and 44 everything here was built by Quennell and Hart. They began with Nos. 3–23 (1900–02) and Nos. 2–18 (1901–02) at the far end by Platt's Lane, and worked their way along the street. The houses mix sequences of detached with semi-detached and several of them feature in Quennell's book of 1906. Perhaps the most distinguished design is the semi-detached pair, Nos. 40–42 which almost match each other, but pleasingly not quite.

The Hampstead street directories of this period, together with other sources, provide interesting sidelights on the way that luxurious suburban developments like these streets in Hampstead were marketed, sold and resold in their early years. George Hart's 'West Hampstead Estate' was promoted and the sales handled by the estate agents Farebrother Ellis (a map of it is in the Hampstead Central Library). The estate agent's advertising brought potential buyers to Hart's own estate office — in 1905 this was on the corner of Ferncroft Avenue and Hollycroft Avenue, where most of his building work was going on, but by 1910 Hart had moved the office to the corner of Redington Road and Templewood Avenue (by then his largest development in

59. Nos. 40–42 Ferncroft Avenue. Semi-detached houses designed in 1904 by C.H.B. Quennell.

hand). In the large hut that formed this office, potential buyers would be shown plans of various houses being built and then conducted to the building sites of any that interested them.

The 1905 directory lists the names of the original buyers in several roads and gives a picture of the kind of people they were. In Hollycroft Avenue they included a solicitor, a surgeon and a retired Commodore of the Royal Navy. In Ferncroft Avenue, the names are mostly ordinary English ones but nine years later there has been a considerable turnover of residents, perhaps an indication that the original owners were speculating and selling quickly, or perhaps something about the new houses and surroundings did not after all suit many of them.

HOLLYCROFT AVENUE AND ROSECROFT AVENUE

Part way up the rise of Ferncroft Avenue, our walk turns right into Hollycroft Avenue. In 1905 the houses along this street were largely completed, though they were so new that they had not yet been allotted numbers. On the right, Nos. 33–49 were designed by QUENNELL in 1906–06, a good quiet series of houses, mostly semi-detached. Opposite these, on the left of the street, is **No. 46**, one of the outstandingly attractive houses in Hampstead. It is not very large but it was built in 1907 to the designs of SIR GUY DAWBER (1861–1938), who was among the most sensitive architects of the early twentieth century. Dawber trained with Sir Ernest George and became well known for his country house designs. His only large work is the Baroque building at 59–60 Pall Mall (1907, but altered), while several of his other houses can be seen in Hampstead Garden Suburb (e.g. Nos. 38–48 Temple Fortune Lane and 20 and 36 Hampstead Way and others, all of between 1907 and 1912).

No. 46 sits on top of a steep little bank, well above the general level of Hollycroft Avenue. It is approached by brick steps up to a central front door and a sprightly brick street frontage. The gable and slender chimney stack on the right are visually balanced by a strong double stack on the left. It is a serene and airy composition — compare it

60. The idyllic Kidderpore estate in Hampstead with plans for new houses by the architects Davis and Emanuel.

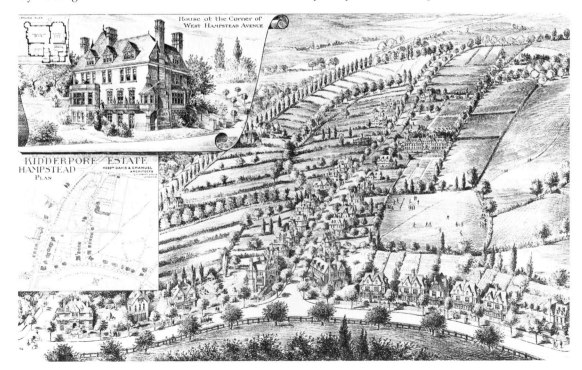

61. No. 46 Hollycroft Avenue, designed 1907 by the architect Sir Guy Dawber. (See previous page)

with its swaggering neighbour, No. 44. Beyond No. 46, all the even numbers and 3–31 of the odd numbers of Hollycroft Avenue, were built in the early 1900s by the firm W.J. King of Heath Street and probably designed by their regular architect G.H. SAUNDERS. They are handsome enough Edwardian houses, but do not call for special comment here.

Rosecroft Avenue branches off Hollycroft Avenue to the right (note the Edwardian and Modern hotch-potch that No. 4 has become) and our walk follows it. Like the other 'croft' ending avenues, Rosecroft was named (apparently at Hart's suggestion) as early as 1896. But in 1905, there were only four houses built in it, at the Platt's Lane end of the street. These included Quennell's Phyllis Court (whose designs he exhibited at the Royal Academy summer exhibition in 1900), and No. 1 built by the firm of Boddy and Chapman probably for Quennell's brother. The other two were presumably the interesting sculpted houses, now Nos. 17 and 18, one of which is dated 1898 across its two gables.

By 1910, Rosecroft Avenue still had only seven houses, but the 1914 street directory shows it largely built up before the Great War began, with Nos. 1 to 11 (plus a house called Wentworth) on the west side, and Nos. 10–28 on the east side. A short route for our walk would go as far as No. 18, built in 1898 (to see the extensive relief sculpture done in a Pre-Raphaelite style on the front of the house by an unknown artist) and then retrace the same way back to Ferncroft Avenue. If a longer walk is wanted, a route continuing to the end of Rosecroft and left down Platt's Lane noting Nos. 29–39

and 18–24 of 1900 to Quennell's immature 1897–98 designs, and other early and very pleasing Quennell-Hart semi-detached houses (all Briardale Gardens, 1898–1900) will bring you to another left turn into Ferncroft Avenue, up its rise and down the other side between the rows of Quennell houses already mentioned, and so back to the same point on the corner of Kidderpore Gardens.

KIDDERPORE GARDENS
This little street was called Cecilia Road until about 1906, when the row of small semi-detached houses numbered 5–23 was completed. These were designed by QUEN-NELL and built by Hart in their most nestling and restrained mood. The houses on the opposite, southern side of the street are of the same period but done by other people.

KIDDERPORE AVENUE — WESTFIELD COLLEGE
At the farther end of Kidderpore Gardens, we are on the corner with Kidde.pore Avenue and approaching the furthest and most impressive part of our walk. On the right, No. 6 is a noticeable house in the Arts and Crafts style of *c*1900, perhaps by Arthur Keen. On the opposite side of the road, No. 9 is a long low house of 1904, apparently the only one designed by QUENNELL in this street. It is an unusual plan for him — normally he had to arrange his rooms economically around a central smallish hall, but here he had the space to use a fairly long corridor to connect them. Turning to the right up Kidderpore Avenue, beyond these two houses all is Westfield College, part of the University of London, founded in Hampstead as the London College for Ladies in 1882 with five resident lady students at what is now 4–6 Maresfield Gardens, near the bottom end of Fitzjohn's Avenue. The College moved here to Kidderpore Avenue in 1891.

Westfield College was the creation of a formidable pioneer of women's university education called Miss Constance Garnett, who remained Mistress of the institution as it grew, up to 1913. In 1883, with eleven students, a dispute over the proposal to call it St Hilda's was ended by agreement on the temporary name College for Ladies at Westfield, a name which survives over 100 years later.

In 1889, now with 18 students, Miss Garnett (largely funded by a feminist called

62. Briardale Gardens, off Platts Lane. A pair of semi-detached houses designed 1897–98 by C.H.B. Quennell. The first of his numerous designs in this area for the quality builder-developer George Washington Hart. These designs, repeated with variations all along this side of the street, show a keen awareness of Arts and Crafts architects, such as Voysey, and the progressive contemporary work of the LCC Architects' Department.

63. Kidderpore Hall, Kidderpore Avenue, built 1840–43. A neo-classical villa designed by an unknown architect for the retired Nabob John Teil, whose fortune had been made in Calcutta. Since 1889 it has been the centre of Westfield College.

64. The old Skeel Library, Westfield College. Designed 1903 by R. Falconer Macdonald. A charming Edwardian building, currently sadly abused.

Miss Dudin Brown), purchased for Westfield the large stucco-walled Neo-Classical villa Kidderpore Hall. The house had been built in 1840–43 for a Nabob called John Teil, a retired merchant, wealthy from trading in army accoutrêments in Kidderpore, near Calcutta. The name of Teil's architect is not known, but it is a dignified design in the tradition of, say, Decimus Burton. Teil died with his estate heavily mortgaged in 1854. After several changes of ownership and some alterations, it fell into the hands of the shipbuilder Sir Alfred Yarrow in 1889, who sold most of it as high-class residential plots. Westfield College bought the big house and two and a half acres of grounds for £12,000.

Miss Garnett then organised an open architectural competition in 1889 for the alterations and new buildings to transform the villa into a university college. This was won by ROBERT FALCONER MACDONALD (1862-1913), later to be one of the successful architectural partners known as Read and Macdonald. Educated in the evenings at the Royal Academy Schools, he also worked under two distinguished architects to complete his training — these were the London Scot J.J. Stevenson and then Sir Ernest George when his firm (George and Peto) was building its great series of Kensington houses in the mid 1880s. Macdonald set up his own practice in 1887, won the Westfield competition two years later and in 1891 formed a partnership with his former colleague in George's office, Herbert Read. Together they later did Stanford's Map Shop in Long Acre (1901), the excellent Nos. 57–59 Piccadilly (1904), 22 Grosvenor Square and many other buildings in London and elsewhere.

In the 1980s, Westfield College consists of a bewildering complex of around twenty buildings of contrasting sizes and styles. To give an idea of the development and sequence, it is best to stand in Kidderpore Avenue opposite the original stucco villa of 1840. This still contains the heart of the College, including the Principal's rooms. Falconer Macdonald's very attractive first designs were executed in 1890–91. Apart from internal alterations to the old villa, they included the new Dining Hall to its right (as seen from Kidderpore Avenue) and the Maynard Wing with students' rooms behind that at right-angles to the road (so forming the first side of a planned future quadrangular court). The style of the new 1890 buildings is a free and gentle version of the Baroque, done in a soft brownish-red brick. Astonishingly (to us a hundred years later), the classical stuccoed villa was painted 'a good beef red' to match the new brick buildings.

The next building is perhaps the most engaging of all Falconer Macdonald's designs. This is the Skeel Library, with a pretty cupola above and a swelling bow window, built to the right of the dining Hall in 1903 (gallery added around its main upper room in 1911, again by Macdonald). This old Library is Edwardian Baroque architecture at its most relaxed, yet characterful and distinguished. It is one of the five really fine buildings in the College and occupies a central position second only to the original Neo-Classical villa. It is therefore all the more shameful that the interiors of both the upper reading room and the large room below have been sadly wasted and vandalised since a separate college library was built across the road in 1968.

Macdonald's last building for Westfield was the Dudin Brown residential building added to the right of the old library in 1905, forming a second arm for the courtyard. In 1913, the year that Miss Garnett retired as Mistress, Macdonald died. The authorship of these handsome Edwardian buildings was unknown until recently, and we have to thank Janet Sondheimer's researches into College records for allowing Falconer Macdonald to receive recognition for them.

A brief record of the other Westfield buildings will be useful here, for they include some excellent designs and their story is not readily available elsewhere. In 1927, a third side of the courtyard was enclosed by the Chapman Wing at the rear, parallel with Kidderpore Avenue. The architect was possibly P.R. MORLEY HORDER (1870–1944) who, with his partner VERNER O.REES, designed the small dramatic masterpiece of a chapel (1928–29) at the far left corner of the garden beyond the original Kidderpore Hall villa. At the time they were also supervising the building of the London School of Hygiene and Tropical Medicine in Gower Street. On the completion of *that* building in 1929 their partnership was dissolved and it was Verner Rees who kept the Westfield College work. Rees went on to re-do the Dining Hall building (1935, replacing the Edwardian bridge building between the 1890 dining hall and the 1903 library), and then designed the Orchard Wing residential building (1936, stretching from Kidderpore Avenue, further down the hill, into the right-hand side of the courtyard). Rees applied here and at the School of Tropical Medicine a theory of proportions based on the Golden Cut — the whole design was controlled by a magic grid, into which the shapes and spacing of the solids and voids were filled. Rees still went on after the 2nd World War to do the gargantuan Queen's Building (designed 1957, built 1960–62), a tower block for the teaching of sciences, on the opposite side of the road. He then retired, which was none too soon for his reputation or for the beauty of Westfield.

In 1962-63, the Refectory Building was put up on the south side of Kidderpore Avenue and the primitive New Orchard residential building finally closed off the fourth side of the original courtyard on the north side of the road in 1963–65 (architect not known).

In 1964 SIR HUGH CASSON was appointed Consultant to Westfield College and his firm Casson Conder and Partners designed almost all the subsequent buildings. These are the four imaginatively linked houses and common rooms known as Kidderpore Hall (1968–72) which serve as students' residences on the west corner of Kidderpore Avenue and Platt's Lane; the fine new Skeel Library (1968–72) also in the part of Westfield west of Kidderpore Avenue; the enchantingly elegant Queen Mother's Hall (1981–82) on the north side of the road between the original villa and the church. Like many a campus of a university or large school, the Westfield buildings form a heterogeneous jumble rather than an integrated whole, but there are gems among them.

KIDDERPORE AVENUE — northern end

Beyond the College, the right-hand side of Kidderpore Avenue has a group of four excellent buildings of the turn of the century, which worthily represent the architecture of the Arts and Crafts movement in a variety of modes. These buildings, together with the early parts of Westfield College, form the climax of this late Victorian and Edwardian walk.

The first two buildings are **No. 12, the Vicarage**, and then **St Luke's Church**, both designed by BASIL CHAMPNEYS whose own house, Hall Oak, off Frognal, was described earlier in these walks.

Previously the local congregation had met in a ramshackle temporary structure on the site of the present vicarage, while the church was being built; St Luke's opened in 1898 and the vicarage was finished in 1899. Both were worth waiting for. Champneys gives variety to the composition of the frontage of the vicarage by open porches recessed into the walls of the house. Inside, the drawing room is a subtly complicated space. Down the passageway between vicarage and church can be glimpsed an intriguing chimney and the green copper of a most beautiful cupola floating over a turret at the rear. This is some preparation for the brilliant effervescene of the exterior of the church. The front gate has touches reminiscent of a castle. Its underlying architectural composition is quite restrained, but the whole elevation fizzes with delectable stone carving and other decoration set off by the soft orange-red brick. The interior is more solemn — brick walls painted white, arches and other features of pale cream stone, with dark wooden seating below and dark beams in the roofs above.

Beyond the church is another notable house, **No. 14**. This was designed by ARTHUR

65. St. Luke's Church, Kidderpore Avenue. Designed by Basil Champneys in 1898.

66. Annesley Lodge, no. 8 Platts Lane. Built 1895–96 by Charles Voysey for his father. One of the most distinguished Arts and Crafts free style houses anywhere.

KEEN in an outrageously exaggerated artistic way, to be the *atelier* of his friend George Hillyard Swinstead, the artist. The frontage swirls and swells with sculpture and Arts and Crafts motifs such as the turret, red-tiled dome and stylised weather vane. There are big transomed bow windows to left and right, and a charming hipped roof. A plaster plaque above the front door carries the date 1901.

If No. 14 makes one smile with pleasure at its extremism, the first sight of the corner house beyond it, No. 8 Platt's Lane, makes one catch one's breath. For this is the lovely house called **Annesley Lodge** that the great pioneer of Arts and Crafts architecture, CHARLES FRANCIS ANNESLEY VOYSEY, designed and built for his father, the Rev. Charles

67. *Detail of Annesley Lodge.*

68. *C.F.A. Voysey, architect, (1857–1941).*

Voysey, in 1895–96. The father himself was a most interesting man, for he was relieved of his duties as a Church of England clergyman in Yorkshire in 1871 for preaching that there is no Hell and no Hellfire. That was a shocking thing in the 1870s. Voysey senior came to London where he founded a sect called the Theistic Church, which preached the revolutionary doctrine of a benign God. It had a chapel building in Swallow Street, off Piccadilly, and flourished until its founder's death.

The house that the son designed for the father was one of a series that was just as revolutionary in architecture. Instead of building close to the road with a garden behind it, Voysey sited the house in an L-plan along the rear of the corner plot so that its arms formed two sides of a front garden reminiscent of a courtyard, and a five-foot high fence along the front completed that impression. The entrance gate to the garden is at the corner diagonally opposite the front door which is tucked into the inner angle of the building's L. Facing this front door from the road, the typically Voysey horizontal emphasis of the two wings makes them seem to fly out from the bold front door porch. The walls are of roughcast rendering painted white, with a touch of warmth given by trims of honey-coloured stone that add to the long horizontals of the band windows. Tall chimneys and slim buttresses give vertical relief and hold the composition together. It is a design that speaks of purity, beauty and originality.

In the Rev. Charles Voysey's time (the directories show him still there in 1910, but his name has vanished by 1913), the interiors were long and low, the entrance hall floor was of tiles but most other floors of plain polished wood, both with Persian rugs here and there. The walls were papered with some of Voysey junior's colourful 1880s or '90s designs for the manufacturers Essex and Co. (later for Sanderson's) up to a plain band about a foot below the ceiling. The furnishings and furniture were of simplified lines and sparse, leaving much space in the rooms.

Outside the front door, the materials and simplicity of the garden formed an entity with the house. Somehow, in 1983, planning permission was given for this marvellous house to be turned into flats. The alterations to the building were done with some sensitivity and the exteriors are little spoiled. But the wooden fence (proper for that period) has been replaced by a wall and the garden has been invaded by numerous stunted brick wallettes that should be swept away if the freeholder does not want to be haunted by the outraged ghost of Voysey. But even that cannot ruin the pleasure to be gained from studying the delectable frontage of the house.

BACK ALONG KIDDERPORE AVENUE AND ITS SOUTHERN END

The outward part of our walk is completed with the great Voysey house and we walk back along the length of Kidderpore Avenue, passing a number of Arts and Craftish houses towards the farther end. Beyond QUENNELL's No. 9 on the right, No. 7 is a nice L-plan house of *c*1900, built as Oak House for Herbert Dicksee and lived in by him throughout the Edwardian period. No. 5 is called The Studio and was originally attached to No. 7. On the left, No. 4 is a big long imitation Arts and Crafts house with black and white half-timbering. In 1905 Arthur Derry lived in it, but by 1913 it was owned by Senjiro Watanabe. Beyond that, No. 2 is Arts and Crafts in manner again, rather watered down but a lot nicer than No. 4; it was owned by W. Montagu Peters in Edwardian times. Finally, back on the right side of the street, No. 1, Birkdale, is an Edwardian house with Dutch gables, done for Edwin Henry Keen JP., probably by his brother Arthur Keen. We cross Heath Drive, pause to admire again Quennell's No. 33 on the corner, and go straight on along Bracknell Gardens.

BRACKNELL GARDENS

Bracknell Gardens was laid out and developed from 1905 onwards. But the first building we see at its western end is the block of flats (built 1986–87) on the left for which planning permission was given just before the Redington/Frognal Conservation Area was designated in 1985.

On the other (western) side of Bracknell Gardens, there follow two very large Neo-Georgian houses, No. 31 (Bracknell Court) and No. 29 (Pelham House) of 1921, designed by RANDALL AND PILE, and built for two wealthy financiers. As an optional side-track to our walk further on along Bracknell Gardens, No. 30 is a pleasant tile-hung corner house of 1913, and No. 28 the sad remains of a Neo-Georgian design (again 1913) now a complete mess from modernisation of windows and other features. Beyond these, 16 to 26 on the left (1910–13) and 17 to 23 (1910–13) on the right are semi-detached pairs designed by C.H. SAUNDERS for the builder W.J. King (some have handsomely sculpted plasterwork on their porches) and then 6 to 14 (1907–08) on the left and 9 to 15 (1907–08) on the right are the excellent Free Style work of the builder James Tomblin and his architect WILLIAM A. BURR (who also designed houses on the north side of Wedderburn Road). Finally, of these houses, all of 1906–14, there is a funny little cottage of uncertain date at No. 3. But around the corner and a few yards down Frognal Lane is **St Andrew's Presbyterian Church**, overlooking the junction with Finchley Road. It must be mentioned here especially for several small but richly dramatic stained-glass windows by the great Scottish designer DOUGLAS STRACHAN (pronounced *Strawn*), rather than for its decent Edwardian Gothic architecture of 1904 by PITE AND BALFOUR.

OAKHILL AVENUE AND GREENAWAY GARDENS

In the 1905 Hampstead street directory, Oakhill Avenue is described as a 'footpath to Finchley Road'. By 1907 it was being developed under the name of Barby Avenue; the first house is listed by 1908, by 1910 it had its present name and by 1912 it was built up. As we walk up its slope from Bracknell Gardens, we can still see how the developers mixed different sorts and sizes of high quality Edwardian houses. On the left (the northern side) there were no more than five fairly big houses in large gardens, Nos. 4 to 12, before we reach the slightly older house on the corner of Redington Road. All of

69. The Arts and Crafts style on a small scale. A desk-top stationery cabinet with bookshelf designed by C.F.A. Voysey.

70. Fire irons and other metal articles designed by C.F.A. Voysey c1903.

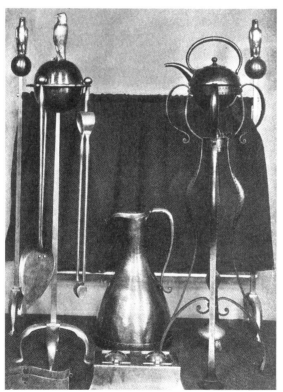

these five on this side are still pleasing, typically varied, houses of around 1910, though some of them have been a bit mauled by alterations and modern infill has added some extra dwellings in the original gardens. No. 4 was built in 1909 (architects HART AND WATERHOUSE), as was No. 8, 'Boscobel' (architects RANDALL AND PILE). The other three, Nos. 6, 10 and 12, are Hart and QUENNELL houses of 1910.

On the right side of Oakhill Avenue, lower priced houses were built in two sections. Going up the slope, first comes a series by the builder-developer W.J. King. There are three semi-detached pairs, Nos. 17 to 27 (all built 1910), of which 17–19 is a particularly ample design in a manner very like Quennell's. No. 15 is a quiet Neo-Georgian work of 1912 on a corner. The architect of 15 and 17–19 was C.H. SAUNDERS, who did most of King's designs at this time and so probably did the other four houses here as well.

The corner in Oakhill Avenue beyond No. 15 is with Greenaway Gardens. In 1913 only one house was listed in the local directory in this road — Frognal Park, whose grounds apparently occupied the whole eastern side, together with the new King Alfred Open Air Kindergarten School. We cross the end of this short street for rich people (named after Kate Greenaway) and glance along it to the Neo-Georgian miniature palaces along its sides — No. 4 of 1914, 5 of 1915, 6 of 1916, 7 and 8 of 1921, 9 and 10 of the later 1920s and, on the eastern side, the swanky Nos. 11 to 17 of the same decade.

Continuing up the slope under the fine trees of Oakhill Avenue, the second section of houses on this southern side of the street fell in a price range between the big plots opposite and the semi-detached series farther down the hill. These were built in succession from No. 11 in 1909 to No. 3 in 1911. All of them are pleasant medium-sized Quennell-Hart houses. After the 2nd World War the great German operatic soprano Elisabeth Schwarzkopf lived in No. 3 with her impresario husband Walter Legge, founder of the Philharmonia Orchestra, and on fine summer nights in the 1950s the air in these streets of Hampstead would sometimes be filled with silver as she sang into her garden in the dusk.

REDINGTON ROAD — southern section

At the top of Oakhill Avenue we turn right along Redington Road. Glancing up the steep bank on the left side of the street, two Edwardian houses stand behind the trees. No. 22 is called Oakhill and was built in 1908 and The Red Cottage at No. 20 was built as his own home in 1909 by George Washington Hart, Quennell's partner in the developments we have seen: no doubt the architect designed this house for his most important patron.

We now leave the extensive Edwardian area of Hampstead and walk back among buildings put up in the reign of Victoria. On the right is **Redington Lodge**, a large house of 1887, built for C. Fellows Pearson, one of several wealthy Unitarians who moved to Hampstead around this time. The architect was HORACE FIELD, many of whose buildings we saw in the first Hampstead walk, in particular in Wedderburn Road. It links the 1870s Queen Anne style popularised by Norman Shaw to the Edwardian Free Style houses of Quennell, with big gables, a fairly strong composition, walls of red brick below, and hung red tiles on the upper storeys. Since about 1946, the house has been divided into two, as Nos. 35 and 37 Redington Road.

Opposite is The White Cottage at No. 18, built in 1900. It used to be quite similar to the house designed by Mackmurdo next door, but was altered beyond recognition in the 1960s and is now of no architectural interest. Its neighbour **No. 16 (One Oak)**, however, remains unspoilt. It was designed in 1889 by ARTHUR H. MACKMURDO (1851–1942) for another Unitarian, a Mrs Geddes. According to John Brandon-Jones, there was a Mr Geddes but it was *she* that commissioned the house and *she* who is listed as the owner, perhaps reflecting the Married Women's Property Act of 1888. Mackmurdo was a prime mover of Arts and Crafts architecture in the 1880s, and his

71. One Oak, no. 16 Redington Road. Designed 1906 by Arthur Mackmurdo, the Arts and Crafts pioneer designer.

1886 house at No. 8 Private Road, Enfield is perhaps the most impressive of all the early signposts to a new elegant simplicity. He was certainly one of the main influences on the young C.F.A. Voysey, though his own career failed early. This house in Hampstead is less extremist than his Enfield design. It sits well back from and above the road, overlooking a sizeable front garden. The central six bays of the frontage provide a rhythmical composition of tall sash windows and a front door of equal width and height. Horizontal emphasis is provided by the strong low line of cornice and steeply tile-hung roof immediately above and the first floor row of bedroom dormer windows echoing those below. Inside the house, many of Mackmurdo's stylised and richly moulded doorways, skirting boards, cornices and fireplaces survive, all originally painted white.

In the late 1890s, the eminent sculptor Sir Hamo Thornycroft RA (1850–1925) and his wife went to a garden party at No. 12, saw Mackmurdo's house and fell in love with it. They immediately made an offer to the owner who refused it, but a little later when Mr Geddes went to work abroad Thornycroft managed to buy it. Thornycroft was then at the height of his career having completed his famous statue of Oliver Cromwell in front of the Houses of Parliament. His initials are carved with a diamond on the glass of one of the bedroom windows of this Hampstead house.

A later owner was Sir Owen Williams (1890–1969), a hybrid of engineer and architect — the Empire Pool and Stadium at Wembley (1934) are among the revolutionary works of International Modern architecture in Britain, which pioneered the use of concrete in buildings. MAXWELL AYRTON, who worked with him on the Wembley complex, also designed for Sir Owen in 1927 the harmonious extensions to left and right of the Mackmurdo frontage and the charming free-standing studio. My father, Douglas Service of the old publishing firm Seeley Service & Co, owned this house for forty years from 1937 and developed a celebrated garden around the house. Later, it was the home of John Alderton and Pauline Collins, the actors, who rebuilt the rear.

Opposite No. 16 is a cheerful Neo-Georgian house of 1939 at No. 33. Beyond that are

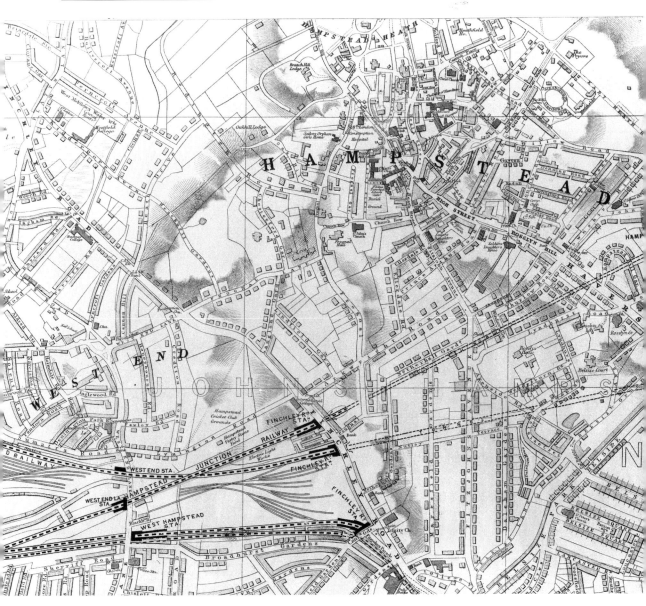

72. *Part of Bacon's map of 1906 covering the Hampstead area.*

27, 29 and 31 in a grim group untypical of the 1890s. To the right, Chesterford Gardens dips away here in rows of tightly packed 1890s houses.

No. 18 has a special interest, as it was the last home of the artist Henry Holiday who in 1927 moved to this austere place from the spacious beauties of his house in Redington Gardens.

Continuing along Redington Road, on the left is No. 12, Wellesley House, built in 1877–78 at the end of a sequence of five houses that were the first in this street after its route was established by the Maryon Wilsons' estate surveyor. It is a big Victorian Italianate house of brick, looking more 1860s than 1870s — now converted into flats, its garden containing two unremarkable 1960s houses.

On the right, Nos. 13 to 23 are a semi-detached series dated 1896–99 in a retarded Queen Anne style, while the detached corner house No. 25 is of *c*1905. Beyond all these, and running to the end of Redington Road, are the vaguely Neo-Wren brick houses built after the Great War of 1914–18 along the end of the old Manor House's garden that ran up the slope beside Frognal all the way from Frognal Lane. No. 1, on the corner, was built as late as 1938.

Returning to the 1870s houses on the other side of the road, **No. 6** is a very atmospheric Gothic house of 1875-76, designed by THEODORE K. GREEN as the vicarage of Hampstead parish church in Church Row. An atmosphere of deep gloom still pervades it. In the front a sheer wall, punctuated by varying windows, rises from the Gothic porch through four storeys to a high barge-boarded gable and a conical corner turret. The right side of this wall swings around under the turret in a rounded curve to a side elevation dominated by a large oriel window. The interior has been converted into flats and the overgrown grounds, where alsations ran baying along the fence to my terror as a child in the 1930s, now contain a tame infill house and a tame garden.

Next comes the final pleasure of Redington Road, the semi-detached pair **Nos. 2 and 4**, built to the designs of PHILIP WEBB. The builders were Ashby Brothers and the date 1876, when Webb was still active in William Morris's firm. It is a long and lovely design, set on a bank a little above the street. The ground floor is of brick and plaster, the upper storey tile-hung. That upper floor has pretty shutters and above it a hipped tiled roof with four dormer windows and tall chimneys. The whole house is draped

73. Nos. 2 and 4 Redington Road, built 1876 by Philip Webb, one of the originators of the Arts and Crafts movement with his friend and partner William Morris.

with creepers and other vegetation, so relaxed and integrated into its surroundings that it is difficult to think of it as architecture — its designer would have thought that an accolade. The clients here were the Chisholm family, also Unitarians, who had been recommended by Ruskin, no less, to use Webb. The architect and historian John Brandon-Jones, who was taught by the great Voysey's son, now lives and practises in No. 2.

On the northern corner No. 71 Frognal is another Gothic house of the 1870s, now entirely spoiled by conversion. With that, we turn the corner up the slope to the left and are in Frognal.

FROGNAL — upper stretch

On the far side of the road, hidden behind a wall, is the old house **No. 88 Frognal**, called Frognal Lodge. It was owned in Edwardian times by yet another successful architect, Keith D. Young (1848–1929) of the partnership Young and Hall, who built many hospitals, including part of the New End Hospital in Hampstead. No. 92 is called 'The Turret', a castellated romantic effort, perhaps of the 1920s. The next house up the hill, **No. 94**, is the long, stately early Georgian house, much altered, which was called The Old Mansion even in 1900 (when the architect JAMES NEALE added the wing) as it is today. Its gardens filled most of the block through to Frognal Gardens (now infilled with modern houses) and beyond. Ownership of the house included a tollgate where people were charged for passing down Church Row to Frognal. Alexander Gray bought it in the late 1880s and began to develop the houses along the new L-shaped road he had built and named Frognal Gardens. His architect was JAMES NEALE, a pupil of G.E. Street. By 1902, the Old Mansion belonged to Alfred Nichols, who had the Church Row tollhouse demolished in that year.

Frognal has a kink in it here. Beyond that, on the left, is the entrance to Oak Hill Park, where a few buildings of the 1860s survive among 1960s blocks of flats and pleasant trees and grass. On the right, there is Frognal Gardens, lined on one side by brick and tile-hung houses of 1889–91, designed by NEALE and built by Allison and Foskett, and on the other side mostly by 1920s stucco infill houses designed by E.B. MUSMAN. Up a driveway to the left at the angle of the street is the house **Frognal End**, built and owned in 1892 by the famous writer Sir Walter Besant, and in the 1940s and '50s by the then leader of the Labour Party, Hugh Gaitskell. It has been converted into flats now. At the far end of Frognal Gardens, on the right at the junction with Church Row, is a flamboyant Gothic house of *c*1900 designed by THOMAS WORTHINGTON of Manchester or his son Percy. Like the Worthingtons, the client who commissioned this house was a Unitarian, an amateur wood carver, Henry Herford, who did all the decorative carving in his own house.

Returning to Frognal, **No. 100** on the corner of Frognal Gardens is crammed with motifs characteristic of its 1891 date — a dome corner (though this one is rather ponderous), warm orange brick with fish-scale tiles hung on the gable walls, sculpted floral panels of brick. Andrew Saint says that the architect was almost certainly JAMES NEALE.

On the left, the old **No. 81** Frognal was a Georgian house called The Oaks, in two parts, altered in 1902 when it was given balconies galore and a roof pavilion, transforming it into an amazing folly. The architect of these alterations was GEORGE HORN-BLOWER and the client was E.P. Musman. It has now been converted into flats numbered 79–83. Behind this, up a narrow path and through a gate, are two smaller houses built in the former garden. No. 85 is a pretty design of *c*1920, attributed by John Brandon-Jones to the owner's son, E.B. MUSMAN. Its original state is hard to read through the modern rendering, pantiles and shutters.

Above this little enclave in Frognal is the Victorian cliff of flats at **No. 97** called Frognal Mansions, dating from the 1890s, and brutishly designed by PALGRAVE AND

74. Frognal Cottage, 102 Frognal. Designed 1906 by Amyas Champneys, a son of the celebrated architect Basil Champneys who lived nearby at 42 Frognal Lane.

75. St. Mary's Roman Catholic Church, Holly Walk, built in 1830. The belfry and aediculed niche with statues were added in 1850.

co. It is hard to forgive its presence in Frognal, with its four vertical five-storey bay windows and their headings of artificial stone completely failing to add lightness to its barrack-like mass. Touches such as the weird zigzag decoration running stingily throughout the façade, and the pebble-dash attempt at 1890s trendiness in the top storey, only drive home the cynicism of its developers. What a Victorian shocker — though its saving grace is perhaps that one of its flats did shelter the great contralto singer Kathleen Ferrier.

On the other side, No. 102 is a delightful Edwardian house, which rather curiously comes right to the street line (while the neighbouring houses stand back). This house, **Frognal Cottage**, was designed in 1906 by AMYAS CHAMPNEYS, son of the celebrated architect who lived farther down Frognal. The frontage has two doors (one for the servants), pretty oriel windows above, and a pilastered central section rising to twin tile-hung gables. At the sides, the lively white gables and their roofs play subtle geometrical games. The conservatory was added *c*1970.

Continuing up Frognal, there are Georgian cottages on the right. At the end of these, we turn right up a steep passage and stone stairways to Mount Vernon, pausing on the first steps to look over the wall at the high Victorian rear elevations of the old Consumption Hospital (with the fine 1920s addition built after it had been turned into the Medical Research Institute — see Branch Hill earlier in this walk), towering above its garden up the hill. Higher up the passage, on the left, is another much smaller building by MAXWELL AYRTON of the 1920s, an isolated outpost of the Institute's research work.

MOUNT VERNON AND HOLLY WALK

The passage rises with a steepness dangerous in snow or rain, and emerges on the corner of Mount Vernon and Holly Walk. Turning right into Holly Walk, there is a tremendous view down its slope, over the parish church and across London. Ignoring some inoffensive modern infill houses, this upper part of Holly Walk has attractive buildings on both sides of the narrow street.

On the left is a pretty group of late Georgian houses called Holly Place, built at the same time as the Roman Catholic church of **St Mary's** that forms their centrepiece. The present white stucco front of the church was first done in 1830 and re-done in 1850, when the statue of the Virgin and Child in a niche and an open belfry above, was added. It has probably been altered again subsequently. The original structure was of 1816 when the Abbé Morel, a refugee from the French Revolution, founded the congregation here. Inside the church, the lobby contains the foundation stone and opens into quite a long Italianate nave. Beyond that is an Edwardian square chancel with mosaic decoration, done in 1907 by G.L. SIMPSON, and a baldacchino and altar of 1935 designed by ADRIAN SCOTT (who was the brother of the architect of Liverpool Anglican Cathedral, and lived in Frognal Way). There are two side chapels. The younger GEORGE GILBERT SCOTT and THOMAS GARNER, both eminent Victorian Catholic architects who lived respectively at Nos. 26 and 20 Church Row, did work on the church, though it is not clear what. The overall effect is very quiet.

Opposite the church is a large house called **Moreton**, designed by THOMAS GARNER (1839–1906), for the antiquary and art collector F.E. Sidney. It is dated 1896 on its drainpipe heads. Garner was from 1869 the partner of one of the greatest Victorian church architects, G.F. Bodley. With Bodley and the younger George Gilbert Scott, he

76. Moreton, Holly Walk, designed 1896 by Thomas Garner in a Jacobean manner.

77. Detail of rooms above the porch of Moreton.

was a co-founder and designer of the important church furnishing firm, Watts and Co. Garner designed this house in Cotswold vernacular Jacobean style, but its walls were unusually (and presumably to save costs) rendered in a honey-coloured roughcast, rather than built of stone. He did use stone — honey-coloured too — in the fine surrounds of doors and the big transomed windows as well as in other dressings. The overall design of the house is strong and free within the manner chosen. The main frontage is on the left side as seen from the street. It has three tall bays, all gabled. The central bay advances dramatically with two storeys above an open ground floor porch. There is stone sculpture over the porch, and a motto 'God is al in al thinges' above the front door. After F.E. Sidney's death, Moreton became an orphanage, then a nursing home, an army headquarters and is now flats. The original gardens fell in a series of idyllic terraces from the front. These were covered with Nissen huts during the 1939–45 war, when the house was the headquarters for the anti-aircraft gun battery on Hampstead Heath, and then sold as building plots. Inside the house, some of the main rooms survived the conversion, including a serene Victorian library on the side nearest the road.

Turning back the few yards up Holly Walk, we turn right into the little lane called Mount Vernon, passing Abernethy House of c1800 on the right (Robert Louis Stevenson used to stay here when in London in the 1870s). Beyond that is a row of six brick cottages built for General Charles Vernon, who owned the top of this hill in the early nineteenth century. In 1900 these cottages were homes for working-class people including a plumber and a gardener — in the 1980s they cost a mint.

Turning left at the narrowest point in the lane, the land drops away spectacularly on our right as we come to the most picturesque old lanes of Hampstead. Walking along the top of this steep bank, we reach Holly Hill with the small green at its top, cross the street and enter the winding lane of Holly Mount. We pass the famous Holly Bush Tavern and a jumble of Georgian cottages, then dive down the first of the two precipitous stone stairways on the left, Holly Bush Steps. At the bottom we pass the entrance to Golden Yard and reach the green space of The Mount and the traffic of Heath Street.

HEATH STREET IN EDWARDIAN TIMES

We are now at the end of this walk, for the Underground Station is nearby. Today Heath Street is occupied almost entirely by estate agents, restaurants and expensive clothes shops. In 1901, the year when Queen Victoria died and Edward VII began his brief reign, most of the present buildings (except the Kingswell Shopping Centre) were there, but the shops and the atmosphere of the street were quite different. So to end this walk we will go down the stretch from The Mount to the station, imagining what each shop was like in Edwardian times.

Beginning at the corner of The Mount and Holly Bush Steps, No. 89 was a builder's premises in 1901, with a bootmaker called George Cooper next down the hill. As yet there would have been no cars, but carriages, carts and the occasional hansom cab would have made the steep street only a little less noisy than it is now. Looking across the road towards the Baptist Chapel, in 1901 there were more boot shops in this stretch of small Georgian houses, The Bespoke Boot Co at No. 84, and another at No. 80. Between these was an ironmonger. At No. 78 was a 'fancy repository' and at No. 76 were the cowkeepers Street and Raymond. Then came another builder, and at No. 72 Miss Pells had an art needlework shop. Below that, the Horse and Groom was there and is one of only two buildings (both pubs) that in the 1980s retain their original trade.

Back on the west side of the street (on the right as we walk down), No. 85 was a second-hand bookseller. Beside him was Archer's the grocer and then the Nag's Head. Below that at No. 77 was the the workplace of a carver and gilder. Mrs

81. Nos. 51–59 Heath Street in 1903. Left to right, up the hill from the old fire station, are Mrs Emerson's butcher's shop (see figure 82), John Crowe the undertaker, Roff and Son the plumber and electrician, C.E. Ferris one of many bootmakers, and J. Messenger the builder and decorator.

Thompson, a confectioner, was in No. 75. Next come three mid-Victorian houses built in the 1850s — No. 73 was a china shop, No. 71 a grocery — and one can imagine Edwardian women servants in their long dresses at the counters, ordering groceries to be delivered by messenger to the houses of their prosperous mistresses — and No. 69 was an outfitter's shop.

Below the Horse and Groom on the other side were three premises before reaching the passage called Streatley Place and the top of Back Lane. No. 66 was a confectioner, No. 64 an ironmonger and at 64a, (part of the building now renumbered 66) was the Heath Street Club and Gymnasium, the first venture of its kind and destined to become Hampstead's first cinema at the start of the Great War.

Below Back Lane, an area mostly taken up by the new Kingswell Centre of the 1960s, the shops down this stretch began with a corn dealer, followed by a jobmaster, a tobacconist, a fishmonger called Nockels, whose marble slabs and shop front, open in all weather, survived until well after the 2nd World War (when the last owner was drowned in the Leg of Mutton pond on Hampstead Heath). At Nos. 52–54 was the draper's shop, Alfred Weeks, where I remember in the 1930s wheeled bronze capsules whizzing on wires overhead as customers' money was carried to the cash office and their change returned to each counter.

On the western side, the shops in 1901 along this particularly steep part of Heath Street were, at No. 67 the central European hairdresser Walter Szolc and then at Nos.

*82. Mrs Emerson's
butcher's shop at no. 51
Heath Street, 1903.*

63–65 the tables and chairs of the Blue Ribbon Coffee Palace. Below that came a fruiterer's, a builder-decorator, a bootmaker and an electrician and plumber. The undertaker at No. 53 was the well named John Crowe, though the building on the spot now looks a little too joyful for his trade, and then there was only Mrs Emerson's butcher shop at No. 51 before the Victorian Gothic splendours of the Fire Station.

The last three shops on the other side, now supplanted by the Underground Station, were dining rooms at No. 50, Macnamara's Curiosity Shop at No. 48 and another tobacconist on the corner. The Underground Station was opened by the great Lloyd George in 1907 when he was President of the Board of Trade. The mental picture of his walrus moustache and leonine head among the crowd surveying the new building's ox-blood tiles and the *Art Nouveau* detailing, provides a fitting end to this last stretch of our walk through Edwardian Hampstead.

Short Bibliography

Burton, N. *The Church of St Stephen, Rosslyn Hill, Hampstead.* Greater London Council, Historic Buildings Paper No. 1 (*c*1982).

Dixon, R. and Muthesius, S., *Victorian Architecture*, World of Art Library (1978).

Gray, A.S., *A Biographical Dictionary of Edwardian Architecture*, (1985).

Jackson, T.G., *Recollections*, (1905).

Jenkins, S. and Ditchburn, J., *Images of Hampstead*, (1982).

Norrie, I., *Hampstead, Highgate Village and Kenwood*, (1977).

Norrie, I. and Bohm, D., *Hampstead: London Hill Town*, (1981).

Norrie, I. (ed), *Writers and Hampstead*, (1987).

Pevsner, N., *Pioneers of the Modern Movement*, (1936).

Quennell, C.H.B., *Modern Suburban Houses*, (1906).

Richardson, J., *Hampstead One Thousand*, (1985).

Saint, A., *Hampstead Walks — The Old Village and the Southern Slopes*; two typescripts of Notes for the Victorian Society (1980).

Service, A., *Edwardian Architecture: 1890–1914*, World of Art Library, (1977).

Service, A., *London 1900*, (1979).

Service, A., *Edwardian Interiors: Inside the Homes of the Poor, the Average and the Wealthy*, (1982).

Sondheimer, J., *Castle Adamant in Hampstead*, a history 1882–1982 for Westfield College (1983).

Thompson, F.M.L., *Hampstead: Building a Borough*, (1974).

Wade, C., *The Streets of Hampstead*, (rev. edition 1984).

Wade, C., *More Streets of Hampstead*, (1973).

Wildish, N. and Hardcastle, J., *Christ Church, Hampstead Square*, (1978).

Sources for late 19th and early 20th century Hampstead building history in public archives and libraries.

1. *District Surveyors Returns* of the Metropolitan Board of Works and the London County Council 1880–1914.

2. *Minutes* of the MBW and the LCC Building Acts Committees.

3. *Drainage Plans* with applications for new buildings (1856 onwards) usually naming the builder or architect submitting them (at present available to be studied by appointment at the Environmental Health Department, London Borough of Camden, Bidborough House, Bidborough Street, London, WC1.)

4. *Hampstead Street Directories 1873–1940*, listing streets existing with house numbers and their owners each year (most volumes available to be studied at Hampstead Central Library, Swiss Cottage, and the 1885–86 edition was re-published in 1985).

5. *Street Maps*. Sheet 2 of Stanford's 1894 Map of the County of London, Sheet 1 of Stanford's 1901 Library Map of London and its Suburbs, and Sheet 35 of Bacon's 1906 Map of London give a useful picture of the growth of Hampstead's new streets and buildings during this period.

INDEX

Entries in bold type indicate illustrations.

Admiral's House, 48
Admiral's Walk, 48–49
Alderton, John, 76
Annesley Lodge, Platts Lane, 71–73, **71, 72**
Arkwright Road, 34, 36, **35**
Arts and Crafts style, 7, 45, 71, 76, 78
Ayrton, Maxwell, 49

Back Lane, 19
Bailey, T.J., 18
Barclays Bank, High Street, 25, **25**
Batterbury and Huxley, 28
Beattie, Susan, 53
Beecham, Sir Joseph, 34
Bell, Alfred, 31–32, 39–40
Bell, Charles, 44
Benson, Gordon, 51
Besant, Sir Walter, 79
Blomfield, Sir Reginald, 38
Bodley, George Frederick, 41
Bracknell Gardens, 73
Branch Hill, 49, 51
Branch Hill Lodge, **50**, 51
Brandon-Jones, John, 34, 57, 75, 79
Briardale Gardens, 53, 67, **67**
Brooke, Lord Henry, 55
Brown, Ford Madox, 43
Brydon, John, 26, 53
Buckeridge, Charles, 32
Bull, Walter William, 53
Burgh House, New End Square, 9
Burlison, John, 31
Burr, William A., 30, 73
Butler, J. Dixon, 28

Camden Arts Centre, 36
Cannon Hall, Cannon Place, 9, 11
Cannon Place, 11
Casson, Sir Hugh, 70
Champneys, Amyas, 80
Champneys, Basil, 49, 61, 70
Christ Church, Hampstead Square, **10**, 11
Christian, Ewan, 11, 13–14, 29
Christian Science Reading Room, High Street, 24
Church Row, 41
Churches in Hampstead, 28, 45
Clorane Gardens, 53, 55
Cobden-Sanders, T., 38
Collins, Pauline, 76
Collins, Wilkie, 41
Connell, Ward and Lucas, 38
Consumption Hospital, 49, **50**, 51
Cross, A.W.S., 30
Cubitt, James, 51

Daukes, Samuel W., 11
Dawber, Sir Guy, 65
Dicksee, Herbert, 73
Douglas, Lord Alfred, 41
du Maurier, George, 48, **48**

East Heath Road, 12, 13
Ellerdale Road, 34, **35**
Eton College estate, 5

Feldman, Marty, 13
Ferncroft Avenue, 53, 55, 64, **64**
Field Horace, 12, 16, 24, 26, 27, 30–31, 75
Fire Station, Heath Street, 21, **21**
Fitzjohn's Avenue, 32–33, **31, 32, 33**
Flask Tavern, 19
Flask Walk, 17, 18–19
Flitcroft, Henry, 51
Foley House, East Heath Road, 9
Forbes and Tate, 49
Forsyth, Alan, 51
Foster, Michael, 37
Friends' Meeting House, Heath Street, 45, **46**
Frognal, 36–38, **36, 37**, 79
Frognal Cottage, Frognal, 80, **80**
Frognal End, Frognal, 79
Frognal Lane, 38
Frognal Lodge, Frognal, 79
Frognal Mansions, Frognal, 79–80
Frognal Way, 38
Fry, Maxwell, 38

Gainsborough Gardens, 16, **17**
Gaitskell, Hugh, 79
Galsworthy, John, 49
Gardnor House, Flask Walk, 6, 9, 18, **18**
Gardnor Mansions, Church Row, 41
Garner, Thomas, 41, 81
Garnett, Constance, 67, 69
Garnett, Dr. William, 57–58
Gayton Crescent, 18
Gayton Road, 18
George, Ernest and Peto, 49
Goode, W.J., 49
Gotto, Edward, 12
Gowan, James, 60
Grayson, G.H., 47
Green Leslie, 22
Green, Theodore, 34, 53, 78
Greenaway Gardens, 75
Greenaway, Kate, 36
Grove Lodge, Admiral's Walk, 49

Hampstead Green, 29
Hampstead Heath, campaign to save, 5
Hampstead High Street, 23–26, **23, 24**
Hampstead Hill Gardens, 28
Hampstead Militia, 9
Hampstead Parish Church, 39–41, **40**
Hampstead Police Station, 27–28, **28**
Hampstead Tower. Fitzjohn's Avenue, **31**, 32
Hampstead Underground Station, 22, **22**
Hampstead Wells, 14, **15**, 16, **16**
Hampstead Workhouse, 44
Hampstead and Highgate Express, 24
Hart, George Washington, 53, 55–61, 63–64, 66, 67, 75
Hart and Waterhouse, 13, 75
Hawthorne House, Lower Terrace, 49
Heath Drive, 55, 62–63, **62, 63**
Heath Mansions, Heath Street, 43
Heath Street, 19–22, 41, 43–45, 82, 84–85, **84, 85**
Heath Street Baptist Church, 44, **44**
High Hill Bookshop, 25
Hill, Oliver, 49
Hill, The, North End Way, **46**, 47
Hoare, Samuel, 47
Holiday, Henry, 61

Holly Walk, 81
Hollycroft Avenue, 53, 65–66, **66**
Hoo, The, Lyndhurst Road, 30, **30**
Horder, P.R. Morley, 69
Hornblower, George, 79
Horse and Groom, Heath Street, 20, **20**

Inverforth House, North End Way, **46**, 47
Inverforth, Lord, 47

Jackson, Sir Graham T, 5, 18, 39
Johnson, John, 26

Keats, John, 10
Keen, Arthur, 70, 73
Kendall, H.E., 44
Kidderpore Avenue, 67, 70, 73
Kidderpore Estate, **65**
Kidderpore Gardens, 67
King, W.J., 53, 73, 75
Kingswell Shopping Centre, Heath Street, 20
Klippar House, East Heath Road, 13, **14**

Legg, Henry, 16, 18
Legge, Walter, 75
Leverhulme, Lord, 47
Levy, Ted, 20
Lloyd's Bank, Rosslyn Hill, 26–27, **27**
Logs, The, East Heath Road, 12–13
Lomax-Simpson, J., 47
Long Edwin, 32
Lower Terrace, 49
Lutyens, Edwin, 49
Lyndhurst Gardens, 30
Lyndhurst Road, 30
Lyndhurst Road Congregational Chapel, 29–30, **29**
Lyndhurst Terrace, 31–32, **31**

Macdonald, Robert Falconer, 69
Mackmurdo, Arthur H., 75
Manor House Hospital, 47
Mansfield, Leslie, 47
Mansfield Place, 43
Maryon Wilson estates, 5, 6, **6**, 7, 29, 51, 53
Maufe, Sir Edward, 57
Mawson, Thomas, 47
May, E.J., 16
Milne, Oswald, 38
Mitchell, Arnold, 37, 53
Moore, Temple, 40, 41
Morel, Abbé, 81
Moreton, Holly Walk, 81–82, **81**
Mount Square, 48
Mount Vernon, 81
Murray, John, 56
Musman, E.B., 79

National Institute for Biological Standards and Control, 49, **50**
Neale, James, 79
Neo-Georgian style, 7
Nesfield, W. Eden, 16
Netherhall Gardens, 32
New Court, 18
New End Hospital, 44–45, **44**
New End Schools, 18, **19**
Nightingale, J.S., 12
Norrie, Ian, 25

Oak Hill Park, 79
Oak Hill Way, 51
Oak Tree House, Redington Gardens, 61, **61**
Oakhill Avenue, 55, 73, 75
Old Mansion, Frognal, 79
One Oak, Redington Road, 75–76, **76**
Owen, Segar, 47

Page, R.J., 38
Perrins Court, **24**
Petrie, Sir Flinders, 11
Pite and Balfour, 73
Platts Lane, 53, 55, 66–67, 71–73, **71, 72**
Pollard, Thomas and Edwards, 34
Pool, Paul Falconer, 34
Pryors, The, East Heath Road, 13, 14
Pugin Augustus Welby, 11

Queen Anne style, 7, 14–15, 28, 34
Quennell, C.H.B. 38, 53, 55–61, 63–67, 73, 75

Randall and Pile, 73, 75
Read, Herbert, 69
Redington Gardens, 55, 61, **61**
Redington Lodge, Redington Road, 75
Redington Road, 51, **52**, 53, 55–58, **58**, 75–76, **76, 78**, 78–79
Rees, Verner O., 69–70
Rosecroft Avenue, 53, 66
Rosslyn, Earl of, 51
Rosslyn Hill, 26–28
Rosslyn Hill Chapel, 26, **26**
Rosslyn Lodge, Lyndhurst Road, 30
Rowntree, Fred, 45
Royal Free Hospital, 29

St. Andrew's Presbyterian Church, 73
St. John's, Downshire Hill, 29
St. John's Parish Church, 39–41, **40**
St. Luke's Church, Kidderpore Avenue, 70, **71**
St. Mary's, Holly Walk, **80**, 81
St. Stephen's Church, Haverstock Hill, 28–29, **28**
Sanderson, John 39
Saunders, C.H., 73, 75
Schreiber House, Templewood Avenue, 60
Schwarzkopf, Elisabeth, 75
Scott, Adrian, 38, 81
Scott, George Gilbert jnr, 11, 13, 41, 81
Scott, Sir George Gilbert, 11, 48, **48**
Searle, C.J., 44
Service, Douglas, 76
Shaw, R. Norman, 16, 28, 32–33, 34, **34, 40**, 36, 40–41
Shepherd, William, 11
Sherrin, George, 41
Simpson, G.L., 81
Smith, T. Roger, 49

Soldiers' Daughters Home, 33, **33**
Sondheimer, Janet, 69
South Lodge, 9
Squire's Mount, 9, 11
Stanfield, Clarkson, 24
Stanfield House, High Street, 24
Stevenson, J.J., 16, 32
Strachan, Douglas, 73

Teil, John, 69
Templewood Avenue, 55, 59–60, **59, 60**
Templewood Gardens, 55, 61
Tennyson, Alfred Lord, 17
Teulon, Samuel Saunders, 28–29, 51
Thornycroft, Sir Hamo, 76
Thwaitehead, 13, **14**
Topham, F.W., 34
Treadwell and Martin, 20

Underground railway, effect of, 22
University College School, 37, **37, 38**
Unwin, Sir Stanley, 51
Upper Terrace Lodge, 49

Victoria Tea Gardens, 11
Voysey, C.F.A., 33, 45, 71–73, **72**
Vulliamy, George, 21

Wabe, The, Redington Road, 57, **57**
Wade, Christopher, 41
Waterhouse, Alfred, 29, **29**
Webb, Philip, 16, 78
Wedderburn House, 31
Wedderburn Road, 30–31
Well Road, 12
Well Walk, 5, 10, 14, **15**, 16, 17
Wells, H.G., 41
Wells Hotel, Well Walk, 10
Wells House estate, 16–17
Wells and Campden Baths, Flask Walk, 18
Westfield College, 67–70, **68**
Williams, Sir Owen, 76
Willoughby Road, 18
Willow Road, 18
Wimperis, J.T., 32
Windmill Hill, 49
Wise, Thomas, 63
Wooldridge, Prof. Ellis, 39
Worthington, Thomas, 26, 79

Young, Hugo, 56
Young, Keith, 41
Young, Keith and Hall, Henry, 45